This book is a treasure trove of ideas and practical actions for mid-level leaders. Often when you're a middle manager, you feel powerless and under pressure from all angles; you are implementing policies and approaches set by people above you in the system and you are under pressure from people in your teams. You feel like you have to have all the answers and worry that if you are uncertain it will be seen as weakness. This book shows how it doesn't have to be like that. It sets out how to take your power as a mid-level leader and make a difference. I've never seen a book like this before, aimed specifically at mid-level leaders. I am going to share it widely.

Dr Helen Bevan OBE – Chief Transformation Officer, NHS Horizons

Practical, insightful and exciting – the approaches and tools shared within will help any manager convert strategic planning and aspiration into strategic execution. It is engaging, informative and really accessible for people at every level to understand how to realize strategic improvements across their organization!

Jason Hookey – Chief Digital Officer, Groupe Atlantic – UK, ROI & North America Division

Practical, digestible and impactful, *Own Your Day* is rooted in real-life learning and experience and should be compulsory reading for any middle manager in any organization.

Alex Botha – Chief Operating Officer, Comic Relief

Working in the middle of an organization is about the most difficult challenge for any manager and this book presents a valuable way of understanding how to navigate these challenges. I like the way it explains why being in the middle is intrinsically difficult and then helps readers to figure out what to do about this. The authors have complementary experiences and present their insights and ideas in a very readable way. It's a pleasure to find a book which is both very well-grounded in an understanding of the way contemporary organizations work and presents useful practical advice for those interested in the challenge of managing effectively.

Tim Morris – Professor of Management Studies, Saïd Business School, University of Oxford

T0272863

Faced with increasing complexity managers are constantly challenged to resolve multiple, competing priorities and pressures. This practical guide distils the best tools, frameworks and approaches to help the challenged manager balance competing priorities and simplify the ever more complex demands of the contemporary workplace.

Gareth Crawford – CEO & President,
Carey Institute for Global Good

More than ever before, how teams operate in organizations is changing. The fundamental conventions of working life are advancing so rapidly that every manager needs a plan if they want to stay relevant. This book is that plan. Blending theory with practice, it's a common-sense companion for anyone who wants to take control of their career. It deconstructs the working day, before inspiring the reader to reassemble these elements into a better, more coherent whole. The first step towards owning your day is to own a copy of this book.

Richard Sunderland – CEO Heavenly

Leading is a tough gig, but that middle management role is the toughest of all! *Own Your Day* gives hard-pressed managers loads of valuable tips to make their lives easier and help their teams navigate these difficult times.

Lucy Adams – CEO, Disruptive HR

Organizational life is complex, and especially for those in the middle of it. And finding your way to the best helpful solutions can feel equally complicated. Good news: *Own Your Day* gets straight to the point, providing contemporary, practical tools and frameworks to help rethink and rework the main challenges facing today's middle managers. Its helpful structure means you can dip in, and take what you need, when you need it. A great way to break down the complexity and take control of the changes you need to make.

Diane Moody – Vice President Organizational
Development & Culture, Royal DSM

A terrific read with practical tips and supportive tools that will enable managers to navigate today's changing world. Refreshing to gear up in the middle, and to optimize leadership impact in organizations.

Dr Hazel McLaughlin – President, The British
Psychological Society

In a year when our world has been turned upside-down, the opportunities for lasting and meaningful change are endless. To deliver on them successfully we need authentic, empathetic, people-centred leadership. This informative and engaging book sets out the practical steps you need to take to make it happen and ensure the best of you and your team is able to come to work each day. Recognizing that I have more power over what I prioritize than sometimes I feel I have, and that I can only achieve meaningful success through developing myself and the talent around me have been vital career learnings for me. As CEO balancing the demands of strategy and delivery is central to my role. *Own Your Day* has helped me to personally reflect on the tools and techniques I can use to make that balancing act a little bit easier.

Caroline Rainbird – CEO, Financial Services Compensation Scheme

A brilliant resource for managers. Comprehensive advice, written by people who've been there and done it.

Graham Allcott – Founder, Think Productive

In a world where everything has changed and the old norms seem woefully outdated, this book shines a light on how you can adapt and succeed. Instantly accessible and written in a style that engages, this will help you focus on what matters.

Rachel Blackett – Head of People Change, Royal Mail Group

People are at the heart of successful organizations and people are at the heart of this book. Packed full of simple concepts and practical guidance, *Own Your Day* provides the tools to bring out the best in yourself and others.

Steve Vine – Director, Defra

In a world where soft power and networks are more important than ever, it is vital that middle management understands how and why to look outwards as well as up (and down). This is a powerful, practical and personal read which gives us hope as much as guidance in these uniquely challenging times.

Michael Wood – Head of Health Economic Partnerships, NHS Confederation

Required reading for all those managers who aspire to be leaders and who have that rare capacity to translate vision into authentic practical plans.

Chris Connelly – Managing Director, Direct Rail Services

I don't think I have ever witnessed a catalyst for change like the one 2020 gave us, and I am excited by it. Leadership will now change to a more people- and human-centric way of communicating and caring for the staff. Remote working will require a very different style in order to keep staff, they are closer to the door of other opportunities. The hygiene factors are far tougher to provide and the relationship between boss and employee must be stronger. It is wonderful to see this book, where soft skills are the order of the day.

Penny Power OBE – Founder of Business is Personal

This is an indispensable book for an often overlooked audience. While most business books focus just on leadership, Julie and Diana skilfully unpack the challenges faced by middle management who are the powerhouse of any organization. This book provides the vital, practical support that managers need to survive and thrive in today's workplace.

Sara Tate – CEO, TBWA London

New light on the
mastery of managing
in the middle

OWN YOUR DAY

Diana Marsland
& Julie Nerney

First published in Great Britain by Practical Inspiration Publishing, 2021

ISBN   9781788602457 (print)
           9781788602440 (epub)
           9781788602433 (mobi)

Practical Inspiration
Publishing

Contents

Preface

It's been fascinating watching the world of work change over the past 30 years or so. There were significant moments that felt like revolution. Others that were a more subtle evolution, sometimes only noticeable after they'd happened. However we got to where we are, there's no getting away from the fact that it is a different place entirely.

Volatility. Uncertainty. Complexity. Ambiguity (VUCA). Changing societal context. Accelerating technological advancement creating this sense of always being on, blurring the boundaries between work and life. Increasing demands for cross-team or organizational collaboration. New desires from the next generation entering the workforce. There are many fine publications on all of these contextual changes. And there are some very clever futurologists willing to predict what might come next in this unpredictable world of ours.

But there is no doubt that the world of work is more people-centred. More human. Hard management principles and protocols have given way to a style of leadership that has people and purpose at its heart. That doesn't mean there's any less focus on delivery, results or success. In some ways, that has only increased. But there is at last an acknowledgement that it is people who deliver this. And the engine room for delivery is the great swathe of those managing in the middle that power organizations.

We believe that no matter how drastically different the world of work is, the same fundamental challenges for managers remain. Those thorny issues that every manager has to grapple with. Things that, if they could excel at, would make a real difference to what they do, how they do it and how they feel about it.

We tested this theory through research with managers across all sectors. One-to-one conversations, focus groups, workshops. Were we right that fundamental challenges existed? And, if so, which were the ones where support from this book would make the biggest difference? We tested some of our early content with wider audiences to sense-check that it had value to those reading it. A huge thank you to everyone who has helped us along the way.

The end result is this book. We've pooled our collective experience of working across all sectors and hundreds of organizations, learning from successes and failures alike. It includes some tried-and-tested tools and frameworks, and some new ideas that you may not have seen before. We've welcomed the input from others. Collectively, we hope there's something for every reader here – practical insights that will help curious managers navigate their world. Our 'so what' test for this book is that every reader can take something from it, put it into practice and it will make a difference.

We've worked hard – with the invaluable support of our editor – to make this a pithy, easy read, so minimum effort is required from you to get the maximum positive impact on your working life. You can dip in and out of a topic area or specific chapter in a self-contained way, or devour the book cover to cover. We don't pretend to have all the answers but have included things you can try which can work in lots of different organizations. We've kept it deliberately concise, but have signposted you to other useful resources around subject areas for those of you hungry for more.

We hope there's something in here that will give you a sense that you own your day again in the crazy world we live and work in. And to do so in a way that is human, compassionate and kind, without compromising on delivering great results. Enjoy it, and do let us know what you think.

Diana & Julie
@OwnYourDay_Book

Foreword

I've spent a substantial part of my career supporting and developing people in organizations. My interest and passion for this arose from my own experience of finding myself in a managerial position with very little preparation, and an expectation that I would pick it up over time. Unfortunately, this is all too common in many businesses. While the world of work has changed beyond all recognition in the past three decades, the same timeless challenges exist. And the need to support managers, particularly those who have come from a technical background as I did, to navigate their way through the middle of organizations, remains crucial.

Some organizations – like my own – are forward-thinking and encourage managers and leaders to develop themselves and improve their performance. But too few do this. And even fewer recognize what those of us who've been working for a while understand – there is no substitute for experience. What *Own Your Day* does so well is to provide an accessible overview of what any manager needs to know about getting the best from themselves and others, illustrated with real life experiences.

Despite 30 years having somehow elapsed since I joined BAM, I'm working harder than ever. Part of that is due to working remotely feeling much more intense. But it's also because I've been leading a team developing an entirely new approach to performance management for BAM. This has been an exciting but challenging project. It's the first fully global process to be launched group-wide – spanning 19,000 people, nine operating companies and in four languages – and a major change for the organization.

As I read *Own Your Day*, I found myself reflecting on some of the chapters with regard to this project. It's gone well, but there are some things I may have done differently if I'd read the book when I started – if only to remind me of some of the things that I already knew from my career but had overlooked in the heat of the moment.

I really enjoyed the fact that it's relatively light on theory and models, but uses quotes from primary research, and case studies from hard-won experience to illustrate real-life situations that the reader can relate to. It provides a plethora of practical tools and tips which will be so valuable to managers at any stage of their career. And it brings to life the solutions to perennial challenges resulting from decades of wisdom and experience of the authors. This is backed up by references to further reading and resources for those that want more. But the principles are clearly there in the text for managers to follow.

What made me delighted to contribute this short foreword was that it responds to the twin demands of managing your own performance and that of others. It's a very welcome addition to the library of books on management practice. By focusing on the *how*, it provides a concise and very readable guide for managers at any stage of their careers. It should be an indispensable companion as a reminder of the realities of managing in the middle.

Enjoy reading it. And keep it close to hand – I suspect you will want to refer to it again and again.

Chris Jones – Director of Learning and Development,
BAM Construct UK Limited

Using this book

W e've split this book into two sections, based on what our research told us mattered most to managers. The first part considers the operating context that you told us exists for managers across all organization types and sectors.

The second part is all about how you get the best of out of people within that context.

There are four themes within each part and we've deliberately written this so you can dive straight into a particular theme or read it cover to cover. The choice is yours.

At the start of each chapter we'll signal what you can expect it to cover. Then at the end we'll provide you with some question prompts to help you reflect about your own practice.

Our experience tells us that remaining curious is one of the most powerful self-development tools you have at your disposal. Reflective practice is one of the simplest, yet most effective ways to do this. Taking time to be curious and ask yourself some key questions is often where our best learning happens.

We've used some icons throughout the book to help you quickly find those questions and other practical tools:

 Reflective questions Top tips and activities

At the end of each chapter, you'll find a resources section which directs you to other useful sources of information on a particular topic, including websites that you can register with to get further details. We've also included frameworks for you to try. Look out for these icons.

 Signposting to other resources Framework

In addition to this, look out for case studies with real-life learning in boxes within their relevant chapter. You'll also hear the voices of the managers we spoke to in our research throughout the text, emphasizing why the things we share are important – you may find those resonate with where you are too.

Part one
Operating context

Middle managers are the powerhouse of an organization, the magicians who translate strategic plans into operational reality. And we all know that generating commitment to a new strategy is best done by involving people in its development.

But what if that doesn't happen? How do you avoid getting stuck in the middle in a way that might harm your motivation and ability to perform?

This section will look at how you can step up and take ownership, be better prepared for what's coming next, influence effectively, and implement change well.

It's difficult to tread the line between being in the know and effecting change when the direction is not always clear from the top and is ever changing.

Manager, public sector

1 Taking ownership

Why it matters

Being stuck in the middle of strategy and delivery can be an uncomfortable place. Especially in times of dramatic change. It can feel frustrating. Like you are being squeezed. Or pulled in competing directions. We want you to reclaim not only your own autonomy in this space, but also be able to create it for others. Whether you are happy where you are or want to develop your career, owning this space is vital. And it's not as difficult as it might seem.

This chapter will chart a course through the importance of context, the impact of your own mindset, creating permission for yourself, embracing learning and identifying opportunities for change.

Context is king

As you take on more responsibility, understanding your organization's strategic intent is an important way of grounding you and your teams in the context in which you work. What routes to that information are available to you?

Strategic plans and priority documents. Board meeting minutes. Live stream recordings of significant announcements. In some organizations, you might even be able to attend Board meetings to hear the discussion first-hand. Taking opportunities to engage with members of the Executive and their direct reports is another way to gain insight and build your network at the same time.

And the context isn't just internal to your organization. How well do you know what your competitors are doing? Who are the leading-edge thinkers in your field? All contextual information helps you understand the direction of the organization, and the decisions made by the leaders so you can provide that context to your team.

Case study: An 'aha' moment on context

As a middle manager working for a bank I was pleased to be nominated for an advanced management programme, signalling the expectation of progression and promotion. During the introduction, the training manager said that he wouldn't be telling us stuff we didn't already know but he would be providing frameworks to help us make sense of what was happening in our roles.

Following straight on from that, Joe Nellis, an eminent economics professor from Cranfield School of Management, ran a half-day session on economics. I remember it vividly as he used a model of a central heating system to help us understand the basics of the country's economy. It was a great session, but I was surprised that such a large proportion of time was spent on this.

I asked the training manager why economics was given so much emphasis when we had an entire team of economists at the bank. His response was that by understanding the context in which the bank operated, I would know what to do in my role without having to be told when the Government made changes to monetary or fiscal policies.

This was an important lesson for me. I realized I needed to understand the company's strategy so I knew what response was expected when changes happened in our market. It forced me to think strategically and take ownership for the direction and output of the team. It encouraged me to share this with my team so they had the same insight to apply to their work.

To keep my knowledge current, I recognized the need to identify the sources of information within the bank, competitors to be monitored, and who were the key people driving change internally and externally. Although the working environment at that time was simpler, more predictable and less risk-averse, the principles of this learning for managers looking to gain insight on context remain as true as ever.

Your mindset, their perspective

We all know that generating commitment to a new strategy is best done by involving people in its development. This creates ownership and buy-in, making it easier for you to then sell that direction to those who work for you. It creates a collective energy and an army of leaders able to advocate for the next steps and galvanize teams to deliver.

But what if that doesn't happen? What if the leaders in your organization hide themselves away and emerge with a new strategy or direction with a grand flourish? One that you don't believe in. One you don't agree with. One that you know will be hard to sell to your team. How do you avoid getting stuck in the middle in a way that might harm your motivation and ability to perform?

Leading a team through something you don't believe in is hard. And if you live it through that lens, it will grind you down to the point where you feel stuck between strategy and delivery. That's not a fun place to be. Pretending you really do believe in it is also hard, and will be seen through very quickly. It also lacks authenticity, which we think is a key principle for effective management and leadership. So the challenge here is how you motivate and lead a team to do something that you don't believe in, while not compromising your own values and authenticity. That's only possible by looking at the problem through two lenses.

Ultimately, as an employee of an organization, you're there to support it in achieving its vision and strategic aims. Whether it is to create shareholder value in the private sector, or activities which meet social purpose aims in the third or public sector. But reminding yourself that it's your role to execute this is a helpful way to frame your mindset as you look to remove yourself from being stuck between strategy and delivery.

The second lens involves putting yourself in the shoes of the decision-makers – a key component of operating empathetically. It's that old adage of walking a mile in another person's shoes. Think about why the senior team made that decision from their perspective, rather than yours.

Case study: Putting yourself in the shoes of the decision-makers

I was part of a leadership team delivering a transformation programme for a global FTSE 100 organization. Like all complex transformations it was a difficult challenge, compounded by a highly federated, autonomous culture, no inclination for compliance, and no willingness from the leadership to frame or mandate. The equivalent of pushing water uphill. But that's what we did, winning hearts and minds, recognizing opportunities for change to prove there was potential for much broader impact, and exceeding our delivery target of £50m savings over two years with a stellar £82m, spending less than half of our £20m budget. In the process, we'd won the trust and confidence of the Executive by speaking truth to power.

When it came to the next annual budget setting round, we were confident that we had enough objective data for our success, a proven track record of delivery, and sufficient political capital to secure a fivefold investment increase in our work over the next three years. We asked for £100m to generate a £400m return. We knew this would not only support the corporate ambition to drive out cost and improve margin in an increasingly competitive environment, but would also facilitate the broader strategic growth agenda. Not only was this rejected, our £20m budget was halved.

To begin with I mainly railed against the perceived idiocy of that decision. Why on earth would they not want to build on the results already delivered, drive that further and deeper across the organization? Why would they not want more of that, especially given how it supported their broader strategic objectives? Then I looked at it through their lens.

They had outperformed market expectations with what we'd already delivered, and their share price had grown as a result. The cultural challenges remained and would require a profound change of approach from the Executive team, which would be counterintuitive for many of them, so was firmly in the 'too difficult' box. Market conditions were very challenging in the UK but there were good opportunities in other regions globally. And key members of the Executive team were on a time-limited turnaround deal. This next financial year was the last one – making significant investment in their final year, for a return after they'd gone, less appealing.

Whatever I felt about their rationale and perspective, recognizing why it differed from mine and acknowledging why it was right for them helped me understand their decision. And most importantly, it helped me frame it with my team. Of course, I'd engaged my team in the proposals we'd presented and that had generated enthusiasm for the art of the possible and high levels of motivation to push on. Now I had to tell them it wasn't happening.

I was empathetic about the fact that I understood this would be disappointing. I was authentic and open about sharing in that disappointment. But I was also able to empathize with the position of the decision-makers. Framing their preference into an alternative future that made sense to my team. Taking them on that journey of being able to begin the pivot to a different mindset, creating the possibility of acceptance. And finally, I created space to engage them in rethinking our priorities so they owned how we responded to the decision. Was it hard? Of course it was. But it stopped me feeling squeezed in the middle. It stopped me feeling like I was a passive victim of other people's decisions. And it enabled me to keep my team motivated.

Creating your own permission

One of the sure-fire ways to end up feeling stuck in the middle is when you can see a solution to a problem and yet feel unable to do anything about it. Frustration levels rise. You rail against all those who inhibit this. Motivation drops. New ideas and creative energy dissipate. Inverting this situation is at the very heart of owning your day.

It's important to recognize the difficulties and how you are reacting to them. What prevents you taking ownership of that particular problem? What prevents you driving your initiative forward? You are employed to create value – for shareholders or society – and you have an idea that will improve or increase this. So why not do it?

Sometimes, having a simple model to draw on which helps assess how you are feeling and what you need to do is all that is required to get into a more positive frame of mind. One of our favourites is the Victim, Survivor, Navigator model, devised by organizational psychologist Richard McKnight.[1] It's a useful way to think about your reactions in a crisis.

> **Victim**: I'm going to drown
> **Survivor:** I don't know how, but somehow I'll survive
> **Navigator:** I am in charge of my boat, I know what I need to do

We'll all have moments in each of these spaces over our careers, but recognizing when you are in victim mode is critical due to the detrimental impact it has on performance, reputation and your own wellbeing.

Often the root causes for being in victim mode are because the barriers often feel like they aren't within your control. You don't have permission, engendered by the prevailing culture or levels of empowerment in the organization. You don't have the resources to implement the solution, granted by the finance or HR teams. You don't have the capacity to spend time on this compared to other deliverables, set for you by your manager.

But that doesn't change the fact that you have a value-adding solution to a problem. It could be anything from tackling a low-level irritation or a game-changing idea to fix a thorny issue. Either way, isn't it your responsibility to drive this forward? A responsibility to your organization and their value creation ambitions? And, as importantly, to yourself, your professional practice, your motivation and the sense of achievement that work brings to you. We believe your approach to realizing your idea depends on the barriers and being able to understand what's driving those. Here are three things for you to consider.

1. The permission environment
    If permission to proceed with the idea is what's standing in your way, ask yourself what that would look like if you returned with a prototype. Whether that's a new process or a new service line. Something visible and tangible with demonstrable benefits. What would that do to the permission environment? It might be that those you are seeking permission from struggle to consider things conceptually. It might be that they're overwhelmed by their own competing priorities and don't have the headspace to think about anything new. How do you make it easier for them to say yes than no?

And if creating a prototype requires input from others, what better way to role-model to your own team the values of innovation, curiosity and continuous improvement, than to overtly sponsor a side project that will make the lives of customers, staff or stakeholders better?

Do it by the power of mass: you can't ignore 2,000 or 3,000 people saying this is an issue and this is how we're going to fix it. Building an organizational network or coalition, a bottom-up dynamic, collective decision-making body.

Manager, private sector

Professor Keith Grint cites the story of a captain taking command of the worst performing ship in the US pacific fleet.[2] He hasn't a clue how to fix the problems but is confident that the crew have the answers. He starts by getting them to solve the badly designed foul weather jackets which they hated wearing. The new jacket design produced by the crew was loved by all who wore it, and had the added benefit of halving the cost of manufacturing. However, the captain was threatened with court martial because the jackets did not conform to regulations. He accepted the consequence of being court martialled for his crew wearing non-regulation jackets, but his defence was so strong that it caused a rethink by the navy. The captain's approach moved the ship from the worst performer in the fleet to the best within two years. He did this

We don't have the authority to make the decisions ourselves but we should be able to spend within approved budgets without needing approval again. Processes and bureaucracy stop things being done and are against common sense.

Manager, public sector

without knowing the answers to any of the problems, he simply asked the crew.

2. Resources

This can be a constraining factor that is insurmountable for large-scale projects, but experience tells us that for most of the opportunities that exist for you to take ownership of, the major resource requirement is time. How do you make time for the creation of a pilot, prototype or proof of concept within the resources you have? Are there team members who can support you and provide capacity to pull something together? If you can see an obvious benefit, use this opportunity with your team to engage them in this. Win hearts and minds. Refine your pitch for when your prototype is complete. If this requires input from other teams or functions, consider how you become an organizational intrapreneur and draw in similarly motivated and like-minded experts into your idea.

3. Your motivation

Be clear about why this matters you. It may be that you had a light-bulb moment, a new, positive idea. But our experience tells us that, more often than not, new ideas are borne out of fixing something that's broken. By its very definition, that will be causing a pain point for one or more people who engage with it. Understanding why you're motivated to take the initiative in this space will help you refine your pitch to the decision-makers. But it also offers you the opportunity to frame it positively. For example, instead of describing it as 'I need to improve this process as it drives everyone who has to deal with it to despair', you could say 'by streamlining this process, it makes people's lives easier, saves time and money'. Make it a joy to work on, with the ability to delight those who will see it.

Case study: A great example of taking ownership

A new manager was appointed to a mental health ward that had a toxic history arising from mistakes that had resulted in very serious consequences. While the senior people involved had left the organization, the remaining staff were dispirited and demotivated and performance badly needed improvement. Recruitment was impossible because no one wanted to work in a ward with such a bad reputation.

On her appointment, the new ward manager met all staff members individually and quickly realized that they felt unsupported. There was no induction process, no personal development and, worst of all, no one listened to them. She listened carefully and started implementing small things that made a big difference, so building confidence in themselves and their work. She then tried new things with patients without seeking approval, small things like inviting patients to try different teas. This became a high spot of the week and because all the patients participated, it had the added benefit of creating time for staff to get on with other things.

When she had built trust with her team, they were quick to come up with their own ideas to improve patient care. There were unexpected consequences from this fresh approach. When the ward manager started posting on Twitter which tea the patients had liked most that day or another activity such as painting, family members and carers began to join in. More people noticed the increasing number of people tweeting that patients were having fun, and she noticed that recruitment stopped being an issue.

Her mantra was that supported staff meant supported patients. She also believed that being transparent in dealings with people was a motivator for them. Sharing this on social media was pioneering. The ward and its manager achieved a reputation for great care. Through creating her own permission in a measured and appropriate way, she tackled long-standing organizational and reputational issues and increased her own credibility and visibility in the process.

Don't fear mistakes – it's all about the learning

In our conversations with managers, one of the most common obstacles preventing them from taking ownership was fear. When you drill into that fear you see that it is largely the fear of getting it wrong. But whether it's trying something new, operating in an unpredictable environment or dealing with things outside of your control, mistakes are bound to occur. And the instinctive response to a mistake is to judge yourself. It could be self-criticism, irritation or a sense of having failed. But focusing on blame and what went wrong leads to a downward negative spiral. Not only is that not helpful, it limits your opportunities to learn. Only by never trying anything new will you never make a mistake. And if you always do what you always did, you'll always get what you always got. As Edison said on his journey to inventing the lightbulb: 'I have not failed, I've just found 10,000 ways that won't work.'[3] There'll be more on how to deal with failure and setbacks in the next chapter.

We believe that adopting a growth mindset is essential for learning. It enables you to focus on what you've learned, rather than worrying about the setbacks. It helps you develop your reflective practice and resilience, which we'll explore more in Chapter 5. A research study into university students who showed great promise but did not fulfil expectations attributed this to them having developed a fixed mindset.[4] This caused them to be afraid of making mistakes and tarnishing their reputation. They had become fearful of getting out of their comfort zone and taking risks, so failed to deepen their knowledge and experience. Aversion to risk is an inhibitor. Collective courage is key to organizational success. So adopting a growth mindset is essential to your development.

Every experience offers learning – even those which seem like a roaring success. Adopting a growth mindset means being open to seeking out learning in any given situation. Take the time to reflect back on the rationale which led to that course of action and the decision-making process – was there learning there? Walk back through the steps you went through. What went well, what could be done differently next time? Look at this as a facilitated conversation that leads to a deeper understanding, minimizing negative emotions and surfacing issues quickly and without recrimination.

You don't want to risk criticism if something goes wrong so you get approval up the line even if you have the authority [to act alone].

Manager, private sector

Recognizing opportunities for change

This is hard, for so many reasons. While we will have a different appetite for change, at our core human beings fundamentally resist change. We've led change of all shapes and sizes from whole organization transformations to incremental improvements, worked as interims where we changed roles frequently, and when it comes to our world we don't always like change! People are creatures of habit. We are comfortable with the familiar. We construct routines which bring us safety and certainty – increasingly so in an ambiguous and changing world.

Now overlay your work onto that. You're doing the bidding of those more senior than you. You're marshalling and motivating your own teams. You're navigating organizational culture and politics. You are thinking about your own career and progression – although often not nearly enough because of the other demands on your time. Is it any wonder that you don't get chance to recognize opportunities for change?

So, if you'll pardon the pun, how do you change that?

It is anchored in that growth mindset. You have to commit to wanting to seek and be open to opportunities for change. Not immediately accepting the status quo, and instead being endlessly curious about the art of the possible. Adopting a challenge mindset. There's a great model from Japanese total quality management principles which suggests you should ask 'why' seven times.[5] We think of it as being like a small child learning about the world, and endlessly asking adults 'why' whenever presented with a seemingly obvious or unchallengeable fact.

How often do you do that at work? So many of the processes, ways of working, policies, procedures or rules are accepted at face value. Levels of frustration are often evident but the willingness to challenge them is not. And even when it is, that challenge tends to cave at the first defence of the status quo. Yet so many of these things have grown up over time, been added to, built on, without anyone ever stepping back and taking a fresh perspective.

Imagine asking the question 'why' in the face of each justification you got for the status quo. Rarely would you need to do that seven times to expose the weakness in arrangements which aren't fit for purpose. Now imagine being the owner of a way of working being challenged in that way. How open would you be to the endless whys uncovering new opportunities?

That approach might help you with incremental change in the here and now, but what about the opportunities for change that are future-facing? Those that require innovation and new propositions that don't exist right now? Those kinds of challenges to the status quo tend to be more heavily defended with reasons why not. Barriers, obstacles, complexity, fear. They dominate. The level of change from the status quo is simply unimaginable for some.

Case study: Are things really too difficult?

The response of many organizations and industries to the coronavirus crisis shows why the fear of change which places things in the too difficult box is a fallacy.

I was Chair of a Further Education institution which offered a range of education and training provision to young people and adults. This was largely, but not exclusively, in vocational subjects, so those that required hands-on skills such as construction, beauty therapy, art and design. In a challenging funding environment, the Board had been seeking ways in which the delivery model could shift to lower-cost interventions, including online or blended learning. The obstacles came back thick and fast: weak IT infrastructure, poor access to online settings among disadvantaged learners, and a curriculum design that did not lend itself to these models.

Then Covid-19 arrived. In less than three weeks, the entire curriculum for thousands of learners moved from face-to-face to online delivery. All with the relevant infrastructure required from support service teams, and due regard to safeguarding responsibilities. Was the quality of the curriculum design underpinning the online offer perfect? Of course not. But it showed the art of the possible when hands were forced by an unprecedented crisis. And it was inspiring to see how the focus on supporting learners was paramount, which was the core of the organization's mission and vision.

I'm not suggesting you should become a human version of a deadly pandemic! But I am suggesting that reminding yourself of purpose and mission is a good place to start when considering what the future might look like for your work. How can you better delight customers, service users, stakeholders and staff with your offer?

And to think about that requires curiosity, plus one other ingredient which is in ever-decreasing supply – time. One of this book's authors was once told that they were a prodigiously productive 'doer', and that approach to work had certainly served them well in the early part of their career. But then they worked for someone who took them to one side and provided a salutary lesson that has stayed with them. 'You are an awesome doer,' they were told. 'But if you don't spend at least half a day a week staring out of the window and thinking about the future then I'll sack you!' It was half said in jest to make the point, but how can you recognize opportunities for change if you don't create the time and space to look up and out? To learn from others. To increase your awareness of trends and the changing external context. There'll be more on how to create that time and space in the next chapter.

What we love about challenging your own practice is the radiated benefit it has on others. As you become more curious and open to change, as you extend your awareness of opportunities that might exist to do things differently, your teams will notice. They will mirror and respond to this way of being. And by empowering them to do the same, you create your own army of advocates all with a growth mindset. That's a very powerful thing.

In the modern world of work, the top three skills valued by companies are solving complex problems, critical thinking and creativity. These are all human, knowledge-based attributes that often get less recognition than technical skills. All of these are prerequisites for change and innovation. Creativity is still thought of as some sort of artistic endeavour, which is not the case. Creativity at work is simply the ability to think differently in a way that results in a different or innovative approach to a task. Developing an enquiring mind – being curious, asking why, and being less accepting of the status quo – will help you recognize more opportunities for change. Many people use brainstorming as a tool to support this, and we've provided some signposting on this in the Resources section.

Questions to reflect on

1. How often do you ask why and challenge the status quo and, as importantly, maintain that challenge in the face of the first refusal to consider?

2. What can you do to create the time, networks and access to information that will allow you to look up and out, and think about the future opportunities for change?

3. How effective are you at role modelling a change-oriented mindset with your team?

Resources

Becoming more curious and open to change

Have you considered how curious you are? As this attribute is so important in today's operating context, try the Curiosity and Exploration Inventory to see how you compare with the general population.

Rate the statements below for how accurately they reflect the way you generally feel and behave. Do not rate what you think you should do, or wish you do, or things you no longer do. Please be as honest as you can.

1. Very slightly or not at all
2. A little
3. Moderately
4. Quite a bit
5. Extremely

1. I actively seek as much information as I can in new situations	1 2 3 4 5
2. I am the type of person who really enjoys the uncertainty of everyday life	1 2 3 4 5
3. I am at my best when doing something that is complex or challenging	1 2 3 4 5
4. Everywhere I go, I am out looking for new things or experiences	1 2 3 4 5
5. I view challenging situations as an opportunity to grow and learn	1 2 3 4 5
6. I like to do things that are a little frightening	1 2 3 4 5
7. I am always looking for experiences that challenge how I think about myself and the world	1 2 3 4 5
8. I prefer jobs that are excitingly unpredictable	1 2 3 4 5

9. I frequently seek out opportunities to challenge myself and grow as a person	1 2 3 4 5
10. I am the kind of person who embraces unfamiliar people, events, and places	1 2 3 4 5

You can see how to score your results on p. 20.

Source: T.B. Kashdan, M.W. Gallagher, P.J. Silvia, B.P. Winterstein, W.E. Breen, D. Terhar and M.F. Steger, 'The curiosity and exploration inventory-II: Development, factor structure, and psychometrics', *Journal of Research in Personality*, 43(6), pp. 987–998 (2009). Reproduced with permission.

Problem–solving

When you get stuck in the mud or are faced with an unfamiliar situation and don't know how to proceed, try Dr Ken Hudson's Ideas Blitz Tool for problem-solving. You can download the template and instructions from his website, https://drkenhudson.com/books-videos/tools

Brainstorming ideas to find new solutions

When facing previously unknown situations and there is a need to generate new ways of dealing with the opportunities or difficulties it creates, brainstorming is a good method to come up with new options. Here are four rules for brilliant brainstorming from the *Creative thinking handbook* by Chris Griffiths with Melanie Costi (Kogan Page, 2019) where you can find all the guidance.

1. Go for quantity
2. Welcome wild and unusual ideas
3. Postpone judgement
4. Combine and build on ideas

There's also a great piece on Griffiths' website, *Why a wandering mind benefits business,* www.strategydriven.com/2019/05/09/rethinking-daydreaming-why-a-wandering-mind-benefits-business

Notes

[1] Richard McKnight, *Victim, survivor, or navigator? Choosing a response to workplace change* (Richard McKnight & Associates, 2009).

[2] Video of Professor Keith Grint on asking the crew to solve a wicked problem, www.youtube.com/watch?v=4E4k2syM9iA [accessed 15 December 2020].

[3] Quote thought to have originated in his biography, *Edison: His life and inventions* by Frank Lewis Dyer in 1910.

[4] Professor Carol Dweck podcast, *The right mindset for success*, Harvard Business Review IdeaCast Episode 283, https://hbr.org/2018/01/podcast-ideacast [accessed 15 December 2020].

[5] *What is total quality management (TQM)?*, https://asq.org/quality-resources/total-quality-management [accessed 15 December 2020].

Understanding the results of the Curiosity and Exploration Inventory

Total	Levels	Definition
10–16	Very slightly or not at all (1)	Focused on own task and indifferent to the broader world. Fears and avoids uncertainty of any kind.
17–23	A little (2)	Prefers comfort of what is currently known. Uncomfortable pushing beyond the predictable elements of everyday life.
24–32	Moderately (3)	Relatively interested in learning new things. Approaches novelty with a degree of caution.
33–41	Quite a bit (4)	Open-minded with a receptive attitude towards new and novel information and situations.
42–50	Extremely (5)	Persist with tasks until goals are met. Willing to embrace the novel, uncertain, and unpredictable nature of everyday life. A desire to continually accumulate new abilities and experiences.

2 Preparation vs planning

Why it matters

There is a rigidity to planning which is incongruous in a much more fluid and changing world of work. Volatility. Uncertainty. Complexity. Ambiguity (VUCA). Changing societal context such as Brexit and global pandemics. Shifting your mindset to one of preparedness creates a foundation for agility and adaptability. It will enable you to better navigate an increasingly ambiguous work environment. It minimizes the risk of being drawn into constant firefighting and allows you to balance the needs of tomorrow with the demands of today.

This chapter will help you become more future-focused through sharpening your own clarity, broader purpose and outcomes, while providing support on how to deal with setbacks.

There's too much planning and not enough preparing managers, from how to manage your inbox to what it means to be a diverse and inclusive leader.

Manager, third sector

Being future-focused

Having clear plans that you can deliver against has been the tenet of many a successful organization. Whether it's an annual operating plan, team or individual objectives that fall out of this, or a specific project, programme or transformation. They all start with plans.

We've been presented with hundreds of plans in our careers. Objective or goal-driven plans. Gantt charts. Milestone roadmaps. And we know that every plan only ever contains one certainty. That is not how it will be delivered. Unless you have a crystal ball, can predict every change in the external environment, every internal obstacle you might encounter, and have a plan based on absolute truths and facts rather than assumptions, then it will be wrong. That's a caution rather than a criticism. It's a fact everyone needs to be aware of. Plans are a best guess of a way of delivering something based on the information available at that point in time.

This doesn't mean that they aren't vital. They provide a baseline, against which progress and variation can be monitored and tracked. If there are significant changes to the assumptions that underpin them, they can be revised. But they are inputs. And focusing solely on inputs, and creating an internal industry to constantly update them, means limiting resources on the wrong end of the equation.

Moving your approach from inputs, and even outputs, to outcomes, is the bedrock of the transition from planning to preparedness. A shift to combine what you're doing now with a sense of readiness for the future. In an ever-changing political, economic, social and technological world, staying input-focused will drain resources on constantly remodelling and reshaping. Instead, thinking about how you, your team or your organization, can be better prepared to respond to those changes will start to build the capabilities you need to not only survive, but thrive.

You can connect with a more future-focused approach by keeping in touch with changing opinions within and outside your organization. But a word of caution on existing data sources or surveys – these tend to lag behind rather than predict trends. You only need to reflect on the series of shock results in a range of national elections around the world to see how out of touch politicians, commentators and pollsters were with the electorate. Far better to get closer to the source of the insight – whether that is individuals or groups.

Social listening, via social media, is an easy way to tap into a range of views and opinions. Joining forums and groups, following influencers, getting content sent direct to your inbox are all efficient ways of targeting insights and views. As long as you are mindful that comments are both subjective and anecdotal, you'll be able to see which themes attract a rapid following. Whether you agree with them or not, this enables you to take a temperature check on the mood of opinions.

Being open to different perspectives and using them to question your own preconceptions is a useful way of approaching preparedness. Many organizations undertake social listening within their marketing functions, but there are tools that enable you to do this yourself which you can find in the Resources section. Consider other ways of staying connected to your environment too – conversations with customers, mystery shopping competitors, new or established, and staying up to date with key industry bodies are all useful tools.

Time to think

Being prepared for the future starts with being clear about your own personal goals. Without this clarity you may well find yourself in roles or leading projects that aren't where you want to be. This will take its toll on your motivation and cause a dip into survivor mode, minimizing your effectiveness. There's more on this in Chapter 1. After years of research into leadership, David Taylor distilled this down to four steps. They appear disarmingly simple even though they are much less easy to do:[1]

1. Know where you want to go
2. Know where you are now
3. Know what you have to do
4. Do it!

Sports coaches often focus on something called marginal gains. This is a theory that says if you focus on small incremental improvements, when you add them together over time it generates a significant improvement. Using this approach to create clarity when there is a sense of a lack of control can empower teams around the principles of focusing on what things can be controlled, fixed or done better.

If you want to maintain flexibility of thinking, you could prepare for a range of outcomes rather than a predicted future. These principles work on a personal level and within teams. Could you use this as a basis to tap into the different insights and perspectives from your team? Gathering views which are contrary to your beliefs is a great way to avoid confirmatory bias.

Case study: A simple lesson in the power of different perspectives

A vivid experience of this occurred when I attended a leadership programme that started with a team exercise.

We were given a bag which contained planks of wood and were told to assemble a single interconnected shape. We were given half an hour to work it out and told that we would then be timed as we completed the exercise. When we took the pieces of wood out of the bag I was extremely embarrassed that I simply could not see how it would work or what the end result would look like. I had absolutely no idea what we were aiming for or how to prepare for it.

Fortunately there were people who immediately saw what the end result would look like and others spotted how the interlocking pieces connected in the right places.

Having stayed quiet throughout the session, it was only when it came to putting the wood back into the bag that I saw there was a way of doing this that would make it quicker to assemble when the stopwatch started.

We practised this with the result that our team was the fourth fastest of all time! While I didn't have the vision, I did have part of the solution to the task that worked brilliantly when put together with all the other team members' contributions.

Unpredictability of work every day, everything can change in a minute. One minute you can be a manager and the next you're a nurse because a patient needs you. You have to be mentally prepared at the start of each day and especially Monday morning.

Manager, public sector

Once you are clear about the general direction you want to head in, and have worked out what you need to do, you will consciously and unconsciously be alert to the right opportunities to facilitate this when they present themselves. You are increasing the chances of serendipity. But to do this, you need the time and headspace to think about the future. Our research told us that a lack of time is the biggest constraint for so much of what managers want and need to be doing. It also told us that those who purposefully carved out time felt much more confident about the future. It could be formal activities like attending a conference on trends in your sector. It might be creating space to work with others on how you might achieve a specific outcome. It could be using knowledge-sharing platforms like Quora[2] to learn from others. Adopting best practice will keep you at the same pace as others, but thinking ahead to the future is where you will start to gain advantage.

Thinking time is the basis of preparedness. How might you delegate, ditch or even challenge current practices to create this space? Eisenhower's principles reframe the classic time management mantra of 'urgent vs important' to show the value of thinking in preparedness and the challenges you should give to activities which add little value.[3]

	Urgent	Not urgent
Important	Crises and firefighting REACTING	Forward thinking, horizon scanning PREPARING
Not important	Routine meetings and email UNPRODUCTIVE	Legacy processes and data FEEDING THE BEAST

One of the simplest first steps you can take is just to protect time in your diary to stop doing and start thinking. Choose a time when you know you will be freshest – do you do your best thinking in the mornings or afternoons? Does it take you a while to get into the zone so you want a good two- to three-hour block, or will short, hour-long blocks of time suffice? Are there times in your organization when you know the demands on your time or distractions like email are less likely to be invasive than others? Thinking about these things will allow you to not only block out the time in your diary, but also minimize the chance of you giving up. Telling other people that this is what you are doing and why it is so important makes it real and asks them to respect it too.

More recently, working from home has afforded more flexibility for thinking time. I put headphones on even if there's no music to really concentrate.

Manager, private sector

Tip to try

Putting thinking time in your calendar is the first step, but sometimes it can be much harder to make it happen. If that's the case for you, try getting a group of like minded people together to share your findings on changes in the market and future trends. Social pressure will increase the chance of it happening, and you'll get the added benefit of hearing a wide range of perspectives.

Once the mechanics of blocking out the time is done there are three key ingredients to gaining the benefit:

1. Be disciplined: you never give this time up unless it is a life-and-death scale emergency. Lots of things will come up that are urgent or important for others that seek to encroach on this time or make you think that you should give it up. This thinking time is both urgent and important for you and deserves to be protected.

2. Be prepared: don't stumble into that block of time without at least some idea of what you want to use it for. Is there a particular issue you are grappling with? Is there some new insight or context you want to learn about? Are there some simple question prompts you can use to explore things with the space and peace to do so (like our reflective practice questions throughout this book)? Or do you just want to be still and present with your thoughts and feelings, away from the doing for a while? They are all legitimate uses of this time you have created.

3. Make it count: having had the time and space to think is great. But so what? What are you going to do differently or what new insight has it given you to put into practice? This is the payback for the investment of the first two steps.

Dealing with uncertainty and setbacks

You might be reading this thinking that the idea of preparedness is all well and good. But how on earth can you be prepared when you don't know what's coming next? Knitting fog. Unknown unknowns. There are countless ways of describing the challenges of making progress in a world that is ever-changing and ambiguous. If you have never been able to accurately predict future trends and shifts in the socio-economic landscape, then you're in good company. The majority of us can't do it either.

The notion of preparedness where we create a state of readiness and build appropriate capability is the best way of tackling the ambiguity and volatility of the world we live in today. Disruption is all around us. Change is happening at a faster and faster rate. And we're coping with sudden and emergent trends which demand a different response whether we're prepared or not, such as a global pandemic or the increasing climate emergency.

Nathan Furr is a strategy professor at INSEAD and wrote a great article in the *Harvard Business Review* on this topic.[4] His research is all about how we develop the capability to deal with uncertainty. It spans every type of person and sector. No matter what organization you work for and what role you do, you'll be required to find opportunities in the middle of not knowing what is coming next.

While we all have innate preferences and talents, all capabilities can be learned and developed. And ones that enable to you to navigate uncertainty are no different. Furr suggests that the heart of this capability is developing a coping mechanism for the frustration that comes from failure. If you're navigating an uncertain world, dealing with ambiguity and an ever-changing set of circumstances, then it will be impossible to always get that right. Framing how you respond to that setback is a capability that will make you more resilient. Furr's research found five frames that you might find helpful:

1. Learning
   There's always learning in every situation – good times and bad. It's natural to have an initial response of frustration, but once that's passed ask yourself what can I learn from this? What might I do differently as a result of what I know now?

2. Game
   Those of us who are less risk-averse might choose to take an approach that games the outcome. Losing today doesn't mean you can't win tomorrow. Picking yourself up, dusting yourself down and, as football managers are famed for saying, going again.

3. Gratitude

   Recognizing the things that you're grateful for is a core part of good mindfulness practice that underpins a grounded perspective and develops a healthy resilience. Being grateful for the things you have helps place the frustration into an appropriate context.

4. Randomness

   Remembering that a lot of life is random, and the best laid plans won't always help you navigate every situation.

5. Hero

   The hero leadership concept of metaphorically running up the hill with your underpants on the outside of your trousers, exhorting your followers to gallop up behind you, is dated in the world of more distributed and collaborative leadership. That's not what this frame is about. If you think about someone who works on the frontline in disaster relief or in other high-risk scenarios, you can see a world where your ambiguity is never knowing whether you would avert a crisis, save a life or have your own threatened. Seeing yourself as a hero in that journey helps navigate that extreme kind of uncertainty.

Relating this to most of our day-to-day work experiences, it's really about how you choose to see obstacles. Many people will see them and feel downhearted – they missed something, it's out of their control, they think they should stop. That's one way of looking at obstacles. The other is to see that you are doing something right – that old adage that the right path is rarely the easy one lends itself well here.

If you can develop a capability which helps you cope with uncertainty – whichever framing principle you choose – it will provide you with stability and a way of navigating ambiguity that has insight and learning at its core.

Case study: A salutary lesson about randomness

One of my first businesses had steadily grown. We learned as we went, developed trusted relationships across our supply chain, and built to a point of significant growth and impact.

Just as we reached the cusp of this, one of our key suppliers went into administration. One day they were in their offices, the next day they weren't. We'd worked with them for five years. It ended up causing the collapse of our business too.

This taught me very early on that having control over everything is an illusion and failures aren't always our fault. I could apply lots of the frames to that situation: I learned lots, I went on to start many more successful businesses – you win some, you lose some! I was grateful for what we had achieved on the way. I try to frame the decisions I make now as interpreting the information I have, rather than thinking I'm in control of every dimension.

Clarity of purpose and outcomes

While we think it is important to accept that control is often an illusion, that doesn't mean we don't need it – both as individuals and to manage our workload – especially in unpredictable times. The kind of rigid control that allowed you to plot work seamlessly from point A to point B is largely a thing of the past. But

The importance of giving people outcomes to achieve and not telling them the way to do it. A good collaborative environment where everyone is working to achieve the outcome and how to solve problems.

Manager, private sector

clear purpose and outcomes can provide a sense of control. And this should be combined with the agility and flexibility to respond to a more dynamic environment.

Let's anchor this point about control first. We know that plans will almost never be right based on the many dimensions that can impact them. But plans give you a baseline, underpinned by a set of assumptions at a point in time. Understanding those assumptions and regularly reviewing their validity gives you the opportunity to vary your course, so you take a different route to the outcome you are looking to achieve. Or even completely revise the plan based on changes that have a more fundamental impact on the purpose of what you are doing. Knowing your baseline is essential to give you a solid spine, a basis for the volatility, creativity and change to be anchored into a point where you can make sensible decisions and choices.

Now let's go back to the beginning. You're at work and you're taking the lead on something. It could be a day-to-day operational activity. A one-off project. A new initiative. A collaboration across your organization or with other third parties. Whatever the desired purpose and outcomes of what you're doing, you can be certain that the course you chart will, to a greater or lesser extent, be unpredictable. Taking the following three steps will help create the conditions for you to manage this:

1. Thinking time

    As we've already signalled, before you even start to do anything, you need to think. Create the time and space to think about what it is you've been asked to do. Take a step back into the big picture to find the overarching purpose. Why have you been asked to do this? If it isn't clear, find out. What is the context in which you are being asked to do it? Where are the potential pitfalls and opportunities? What does a good outcome look like? What are the different options to getting to the end goal? If this is outside of your area of experience, whose brainpower and expertise do you need to tap into to get the answers to these questions?

    Depending on the complexity of the task, this process might take half an hour, it might take days. But it is the bedrock of being able to manage the uncertainty that will follow, and enable you to have a sense of being able to remain in control of what is happening.

2. Create your own clarity

    Your thinking time will have given you valuable insights and information. Some will be individual, objective facts. Some will be subjective opinions. Some will be dependent views based on consequential thinking; for example, if A happens then we'll need B, but if X happens we'll need Y. When you're charting your way through choppy waters, you want a route map which is fact-based. When you have a combination of facts, opinions and dependencies, you're creating a set of assumptions as your foundation. That's fine. It's the way things are done in an uncertain world. Those assumptions are your facts. As we said earlier, they're your anchor points.

3. Make every decision count

    Decisions are only ever as good as the information that underpins them. In the modern world of work, that information will be a combination of sources that you have degrees of confidence in. That isn't the issue. Understanding what they are and where that level of confidence lies is what's important. If you've followed the first two steps, you'll have started your journey with a well thought through approach, informed by experience, evidence and quality thinking time. You'll have documented all of the assumptions underpinning your chosen route map to deliver your purpose and outcomes. Now you're underway.

Those assumptions – including factual ones – will be challenged and changed on the way. Having a process that regularly reviews them, assesses the environment in which you're operating, validating or updating them as you learn, is at the heart of agility. Changing direction or tactics is fine, so long as you're crystal clear about *why* you're doing it. It's a bit like those books that were around when we were younger. You would read a chapter in an adventure and have a choice about what you did next. Whatever you chose would take you to a different chapter. A brilliant concept, it allowed you to get multiple stories out of the same text. But it was also a mechanism that allowed you to track the consequences of each choice you made and what you learned.

It's exactly the same principle that allows you to navigate uncertainty while staying focused on your purpose and outcomes – tracking the changes in your assumptions and being prepared to respond to the consequences of that change. It's another facet of a growth mindset and a way of operating which requires role modelling with your team too. Success is only ever delivered through people, and we'll spend more time looking at this in the second part of this book. As well as adopting this approach yourself, you also need to create the confidence in your team to do the same. When the work on a task is distributed, you need a culture where challenging assumptions with new information or insight, and course correcting accordingly, is seen as a strength not a weakness. A choice which protects the ability to deliver on the overall purpose and outcomes you aspire to.

Case study: A lesson in the risks of not tracking the impact of your changing assumptions

There is a Government agency that makes payments to farmers as part of an EU subsidy scheme. It's the kind of unexciting job that goes unseen as part of our national infrastructure.

Change was afoot in the public sector. The Gershon Review had challenged all organizations to find significant head-count reductions as part of the desire to see a reduction in the Government payroll. All Central Government departments were required to submit a response.

This agency wasn't covered by the recommendations. Not only that, it was in the middle of the most significant change to their policy landscape in the area of farming subsidies, and was in the process of trying to understand that impact, considering the new processes to be designed, and committing to shifting much of their previously paper-based activities online.

Past and current experience indicated that the politics and bureaucracy involved in changing the policy framework in this area was complex. Certainty about outcomes would be received very late in the day, creating ambiguity in the development of the processes and IT systems required.

The leadership team could have parked Gershon in the 'not for us' category and stayed focused on the changes they were already implementing. Instead, they chose to start to see certainty where there was none. Their 4,500-strong workforce would be reduced anyway with the advent of a more automated process. The significant investment case in the new IT was predicated on those savings. But they were taking a linear approach to building the new system, committing to creating functionality before policy and process answers were clear, heightening the risk of it being wrong.

Despite that level of uncertainty, they offered to reduce their headcount by just over 1,700 people. This decision failed to recognize the true levels of uncertainty and ambiguity in which they were operating. It lacked consequential thinking. That would be bad enough, but they chose to make that headcount reduction programme a voluntary one, which only served to compound the situation.

As someone once said to me, 20% of your workforce are your stars, 60% are your Ronseal employees – they come in, do what's asked of them, keep the wheels turning, are the engine room of your organization – and 20% could never turn up again and you probably wouldn't miss them. Whenever you offer voluntary redundancy programmes, you tend to attract those in the star or Ronseal categories. People who are confident they would find a role elsewhere.

But then they decided to run that scheme before they'd got any certainty about the changing policy landscape, choosing not to revisit what were untested assumptions. Pretty much all of their stars and most of their Ronseal employees left the organization and capability levels plummeted.

The uncertainty around the policy landscape crystallized into a collection of unexpected changes, rendering much of the expensive new IT system obsolete. They were suddenly in big trouble and needed their best people to get them out of it... and they'd let them all leave.

The learning from this situation is that when it comes to making decisions, be wary of not revisiting assumptions. Doing so will help you think about consequential and compounded risk profiles when managing your way through uncertainty. Taking time to do this with some good scenario planning will help you avoid the disaster that this formerly stable organization found itself in.

Questions to reflect on

1. How often do you create the space and time to prepare appropriately for any given task versus getting stuck in straight away?

2. How well do you respond to adversity or setbacks? Is that about who you are or how you approach your work?

3. How do you create the time in your work to review and understand any changes in your assumptions and approach?

Resources

Dealing with setbacks

Setbacks are an essential part of working with uncertainty and ambiguity which may cause fear and anxiety. These are natural reactions and if they become unmanageable, try these five steps:

1. **Imagine a better outcome, part 1.** Ignore what has happened and think of what might have been. Work back from that point so you can think about what you might have done differently. Where were there pivotal points that could have had a deciding impact on reaching your outcome?

2. **Imagine a better outcome, part 2.** Now do the same again. This will avoid you falling into any of your own subjective bias, even when considering things in hindsight. The added advantage is that it tests the new assumptions you created in your first imagined better outcome. It also helps highlight the complexity in the causes of where you ended up – there are many consequential steps that contribute to a conclusion.

3. **Imagine a different path leading to the same outcome.** Now go back to where you did end up and think about other ways that you might have got to the same place, rather than a different one. This is as valuable to your learning as it highlights potential pitfalls that you didn't encounter but may have created the same outcome. This will help you be better prepared with this insight for future activities.

4. **Imagine the same path leading to a different outcome.** Now go back to where you ended up and think of whether a better or worse outcome could have come from exactly what happened. This is important to highlight how randomness has a part to play – a small thing might have a big impact on where you ended up. Things outside of your control or within the wider context often have more influence than you think and doing this step will increase your awareness of how to mitigate them for next time.

5. **Imagine a worse outcome.** This is great to make you feel better about having avoided an even worse position. But there is also valuable learning here on the things that went well or the judgment you deployed that you want to use again in future situations.

Source: Neal J. Roese, '5 steps to help yourself recover from a setback', *Harvard Business Review* (2016), https://hbr.org/2016/12/5-steps-to-help-yourself-recover-from-a-setback [accessed 15 December 2020].

Social listening

Social listening is where you can pick on emerging or prevailing sentiments. Social Mention (http://socialmention.com) offers a limited free service where you can specify a search term such as an organization, person or any other term. For other services, search 'social listening tools'.

Gathering insights

You can also identify and follow thought leaders and social influencers on platforms such as LinkedIn, Twitter and Facebook. Joining relevant groups and forums is another way of listening to what people are saying and gaining insights.

Notes

[1] David Taylor, *The naked leader* (Bantam Books, 2003).

[2] *The Q&A website*, www.quora.com [accessed 15 December 2020].

[3] *Eisenhower's time management matrix*, www.eisenhower.me/eisenhower-matrix [accessed 15 December 2020].

[4] Nathan Furr, 'You're not powerless in the face of uncertainty', *Harvard Business Review online* (2020), https://hbr.org/2020/03/youre-not-powerless-in-the-face-of-uncertainty [accessed 15 December 2020].

3 Influencing for impact

Why it matters

The ability to get things done needs a broader power base than the authority derived from a job title, particularly as formal and informal partnerships with other organizations are increasingly used to deliver outcomes. Soft power is becoming more important than traditional hierarchies in the modern world of work. Matrix working across teams within organizations is common-place. Being able to influence effectively is a core skill for your career. Those people who get on have the ability to make things happen coupled with the skills to build personal relationships that inspire confidence in others.

Organizations often have an old-fashioned linear bureaucratic structure/governance but the expectation is agile and flexible which is why companies find it so hard to adapt to a VUCA [volatile, uncertain, complex, ambiguous] environment.

Manager, public sector

This chapter explores the types of power you encounter in organizations, the essential tenets of knowing your audience, building your own reputation and arguments, and the crucial importance of context and timing.

Old vs new power

Understanding the changing nature of power and influence is vital as hierarchies become flatter and collaborating or working in partnership becomes commonplace. And as new power becomes the norm, the levers that allow you to exercise that influence are changing.

One of the main disrupters of the power dynamic has been social media. These platforms have created opportunities to connect and be heard. Influencers in all sectors are now seen as valuable sources of knowl-edge. This has had a ripple effect into organizations where employees expect to have a voice and for their views to be taken into account. This is a contributing factor to the trend for a decreasing respect for authority in general and will be an uncomfortable new paradigm for those who still rely on the command and control power base.

But the nature of power in organizations is definitely changing and new power, as described by Timms and Heimans, highlights the changes in values and the resulting behaviours.

Old power	New power
Formal structure and controlling management	Networked relationships and enabled management
Top-down decision-making	Front line decision-making wherever possible
Competitive, exclusive rights of use	Collaborative, sharing access and rights
Confidentiality, controlled communication	Transparency, two-way communication

Adapted from Timms and Heimans[1]

Understanding the dynamics of power and influence is especially important when you are working in collaboration, as formal authority is likely to reside outside the team. It is vital that you learn to function effectively in this new power dynamic. The primary levers for effective working are no longer status or seniority. They are about reputation and relationships that create the visibility and credibility you need to influence impactfully.

People get around processes and subversion in large organizations is legend, so power can be illusory.

Manager, third sector

Knowing your audience

It's interesting to us that so many people tackle the subject of influencing from the starting point of what you say. We believe that the most effective influencing strategies start with listening. Taking time to understand the perspective and needs of your audience – whether an individual or group – increases the impact significantly. It allows you to frame your points in their context, demonstrating value that will help them, and leads to a higher likelihood of acceptance.

Every individual in an organization is grappling with their own challenges, and bumping up against people who help or hinder them in their aims. They're also operating in a prevailing culture where implicit and explicit levers and incentives exist, which manifest themselves in day-to-day behaviours. By listening, you can position yourself as helping them, while also helping yourself. This works with peers, team members and senior stakeholders. As you build trust and confidence, that will allow you to start to speak truth to power and extend the reach of your influence even further.

If you need to influence someone to see things from your perspective, it means you are inherently faced with the challenge of overcoming resistance. Understanding the provenance of that resistance is key. What is it that has informed that opinion? And where did that come from – this organization or others? What is that individual's learned experience which underpins their behaviour in the here and now? There are very simple conversational techniques that can be used to elicit that information, without asking those specific questions. A series of open, curious, enquiring questions will provide insights – both in terms of what they say and how they say it. Triangulating what you hear with views from others – with the appropriate caution regarding any subjectivity in those views – will help you form a firmer view on the best strategy for influencing them. Complement this with other reference points from researching more about your audience – speeches, articles, online posts and other sources of information – and this will help you build a picture about what matters to them.

You should focus these efforts on those stakeholders that have the power to significantly impact your work. Identify who they are, their interests and the extent of their influence. You can do this informally or you could use a stakeholder analysis tool to help you understand this. In our experience, it is always better to spend time up front understanding your audience's perspective and concerns. Engaging them early avoids frustration, delay and rework further down the line.

Case study: Influencing for impact

While working on the London 2012 Olympic and Paralympic Games, I was part of the transport leadership team. I only joined in October 2011 and, for a whole collection of reasons outside of the control of those there, the team were a long way behind where they needed to be. Functional areas in an Olympics start their planning four years prior to the event and things are locked down with a year to go. The transport team's plans weren't finalized and their operation started earlier, with support for athletes in pre-Games training.

One of my first jobs was to get the workforce modelling right. Numbers, mix (volunteer and paid) and types of capability. The answer was 23,000 people. Yet on the existing planning spreadsheet for all the areas, there were just 100 people for transport. And the only way to change that was to go to a meeting where senior decision-makers approved (or not) any variance to resources and budget. This was going to be a big ask, and I was new, so I lacked credibility.

With limited access to, and time with those senior stakeholders to build rapport and understand their needs, I tapped into their direct reports – my peers – to gather that intelligence. I built a picture of what they thought of the transport function, what they were worried about, what they needed. The common theme was the fear that the delays to our work were going to cause significant disruption and rework for their finalized plans.

I then leveraged the experience of those who'd worked on previous Olympics on the team. What were the normal benchmarks for transport workforce? Where did that sit in the context of other teams? And how did our bottom-up modelling for our venue footprint and requirements compare? Importantly, I used this process to then get the support of their direct reports, using the evidence base to provide credibility for our request.

On the timing point, I had very little control over this. We were so far behind, every moment counted. And the meeting that made these decisions sat at a predetermined frequency. But I did have the context of urgency to resolve this and the challenges it would create for others.

I chose to take my peers from the other teams into the room with me, providing advocacy and evidence to their Directors that they had been appropriately engaged and were supportive of the recommendation. But even with this, the ask was significant. It would create additional work for almost every other area – uniforms, accommodation, training, catering – and add significant cost.

It was apparent that, even with the advocacy and the evidence base, the timing was dreadful. The vested interests of people around the table, also under significant pressure to deliver, were going to be hard to shift. There was only one common goal – to ensure a successful Games. And there was only one way to focus on that – using evidence and comparators from other Games.

Because I was confident in the evidence base and the support from the advocates I had brought into the room, I took a risk of highlighting their role in having made the problem to create complicity in finding the solution. I used the analogy of a birthday party, where there's a cake, and everyone goes to get a piece, and no one wants to be the person who takes the last piece, so what's left gets smaller and smaller.

I pointed out that is what had happened before the transport team belatedly joined. Every other area had claimed its part of the cake, helping itself. That those people in the room with prior Olympic experience knew that what was left wasn't sufficient for the second largest operational area in any Games. But they'd chosen to ignore that, and protect their own interests. So, yes, transport was here with a problem. But it wasn't a problem of our making. And more importantly, we had a solution too. One which required everyone to pitch in.

Holding that mirror up and speaking truth to power was the only way of getting the decision we needed in the time we had. It was a risky strategy, but was only made possible because of the time I'd taken to understand what was driving my audience, what worried them and preparing a strong evidence base.

Building reputation and visibility

Building profile and influence is key to success. This has traditionally been achieved through the effective direct influencing of key stakeholders. But in a world of soft power, informal networks and other routes to raising your profile are as important. One of the best ways to do this is to build trusted, credible relationships with executive assistants and other gate-keepers that can facilitate access to senior stakeholders. This kind of endeavour takes consistent time and effort and should be planned into your working pattern to ensure the best results.

As with all good plans, identifying requirements before rushing to solutions is key. Define what visibility means to deliver your outcome. Is it face-to-face time? If so, is that a one-off or ongoing require-ment? Or is it about opportunities to shine in settings where your target stakeholders will be present? Or is it about formal or informal networking opportunities? These all require different strategies and have different constraints. Face-to-face time will be hard to secure and likely to have a long lead time for the first meeting. Opportunities to shine may not naturally occur, and may require several steps to reach that point. Networking opportunities may be afforded by your orga-nization, or you may need to look beyond those boundaries. Clarity about what's required and how you might obtain it is fundamental to your preparedness.

Why is it that you want or need that visibility? What outcome are you trying to achieve? Understanding that first will allow you to be targeted as to which stakeholder and why. It could be someone you want to learn from. It could be someone you want to impress with one eye on a future move. It could be part of a current project you're working on which they are sponsoring or are interested in. Whatever the outcome, clarity on that will mean you invest the limited time that you both have wisely, and engage in the process authentically.

Case study: Understanding the Board

One of our network shared how they gained a better under-standing of her Board. She built really strong one-to-one rela-tionships with all the key decision-makers, particularly the

Managing Director, Retail Director, Customer Director and Finance Director. She did this over a number of years via regular one-to-one sessions where she listened to their concerns, understood what they needed to know about the market, competitors or their customers to inform their decisions, delivering that information in a way which they and their teams could act on. She discovered that the Managing Director and her boss, the Customer Director, were both really keen to be customer-focused and make evidence-led decisions, so that insight enabled her to get regular airtime as well as visibility with the Board as she represented the voice of the customer.

Being familiar with your organization's strategic aims and having relevant external information will be noted by stakeholders. Being connected externally with individuals you have met at conferences or events, or maintaining relationships with people you have worked with in the past is a valuable way to build your reputation. What is often overlooked is that being favourably commented on by people outside your organization has a very powerful effect on internal colleagues and stakeholders. Social media can support this alongside face-to-face encounters. Look for opportunities to meet senior stakeholders and when you're going to see them face-to-face, prepare what you would like them to know about you and how you might be able to help them, in addition to the usual research on their interests.

Having a strong LinkedIn profile is a must, even in the public sector, and creating a following on Twitter shows you to be an influencer whom others will take note of. Never mix work and your personal life on social media. There are countless people who have got into trouble and at the very least suffered from sleepless nights due to this. Others have lost their jobs. From our research, the most common separation was using LinkedIn and Twitter for work keeping Facebook

People come to me and say 'I know you can get things done.' It's about having the relationships and maintaining them. If you've got a reputation for delivering in the past you will be asked again and sometimes it is people whose opinions are valued, which counts for a lot.

Manager, public sector

and Instagram for personal use. We recognize that this separation is more difficult for people in creative companies for whom the visual dimension of Facebook and Instagram are critical to their business platforms, but this can be managed through distinctive personal and business accounts.

Building a compelling argument

Now you know who you are targeting and the reason for their resistance, what is it that you have to do to counteract that? How well evidenced is your argument? How does it help your audience with their problems? What's in it for them? How can you create advocacy ahead of the ask? Critical to success is the need for a strong shared purpose, underpinned by a participatory and open approach.

Case study: How shared purpose creates advocacy

During a merger process where I was leading a project to create a new customer proposition, a situation developed where the IT teams from both organizations would not meet up or even be in the same room as each other. They were both stuck in the 'my system is better than yours' mindset and finding agreement on future needs was proving impossible. Both groups were convinced that their system, the one they knew well, was the best one and did not take kindly to criticism from the other company. Though they did not say anything, they were concerned about their own personal futures. This was preventing them seeing the opportunity to do something completely new in the market.

However, once the new proposition had been agreed and they had a shared vision of the future, cooperation quickly followed, with the recognition of the potential for the organization with a pioneering new IT system. Using a common purpose centred on customer requirements provided an objective measure for assessing what success looked like.

Collaborating with competitors requires us to think about relationships in a different light, recognizing the skills and capabilities needed to support this way of working. This is a major change for many managers and one that frequently makes them uncomfortable. It requires a different sort of language from the combative, war-inspired vocabulary so often used in business – 'defending market share', 'it's a minefield' or 'on the front line'.

In addition to thinking about how you make your case in the context of their wants and needs, think about your pitch. You may have gone through a thought process that leads to your conclusion, but rehearsing that sequentially with your audience misses the opportunity. Think like a journalist. Give them the headline. Then a tagline that supports the headline. Then signal that you have more to share if they're interested. This is where clarity has the biggest impact on success.

It's important to make the case – some companies are very good at evaluating effectiveness of expenditure while others are not.

Manager, private sector

For example:

- I've got a solution to the problem which Team X have been grappling with.
- I've validated it with all the relevant people and that's why I'm confident it can work.
- We've worked it up in some detail to ensure that there aren't any insurmountable issues.

That's so much more compelling than a meandering journey starting with why you had your idea, how you went about working up your proposal, everyone you spoke to on the way and finally arriving at the punchline!

And of course you might not get what you want first time. There might be a process of negotiation. Given how much more engagement there is with colleagues it surprises us how negotiation is not recognized as a valuable tool for securing support, and nor is it a core part of any training or development programme. Most successful negotiations are predicated on this principle of common objectives, or a win–win solution. Without this approach all you get is the two sides digging in on their respective positions resulting in a frustrating time-wasting battle. Worse still, it can harm long-term relationships.

The excellent book on negotiation *Getting to yes,* by Roger Fisher and William Ury, contains a simple approach which focuses on the outcome, making it a constructive process;[2]

- Focus on interests not positions; have a clear vision of the outcome you're aiming for.
- Separate the people from the problem.
- Create options for mutual gain.
- Use objective criteria as the basis for an outcome.

The importance of context and timing

Context and timing trumps all the insight and preparation you can do. It doesn't make the preceding stages irrelevant – quite the opposite – but if you misjudge the context you may end up missing your opportunity. There'll be an optimum time to have the conversation and that's the timing that works for your audience, not for you. This can be frustrating, and you might disagree. But there's no point wasting your pitch in a moment where, no matter how great it is, it will never land.

When you get your opportunity, you want to be crystal clear what value it is you are trying to demonstrate. This is multi-faceted. It might be your value in terms of your capabilities that you want to showcase. It might be their value to you and how you would like to learn from them. Whatever that value proposition is, have it clearly defined and ready to articulate openly when the opportunity arises. That value will resonate more or less with your stakeholder based on context and timing. Once you know what it is, pick your moment for maximum impact.

Engaging effectively might also be supported by you demonstrating some vulnerability. Whatever the organizational culture or preferences of the individuals required, status confers a power dynamic. This needs acknowledging. And it's a good route into engaging with your stakeholder authentically. Build a rapport based on transparency and mutual benefit by asking questions of them and connecting with them empathetically. When you frame your desired outcome, do so with humility and recognize the situation you're in and how you might both benefit. Be open about your learning journey and why this matters to you. Show your whole self in how you engage with your stakeholder.

Wilson Mizner said 'Be nice to people you meet on the way up as you'll meet them on the way down.'[3] Other than it being common decency, reciprocity is a social norm. When someone does something for you, you feel obliged to return that favour. This isn't time-limited. If you make your request at a later date, that person will still be happy to comply. Done authentically, reciprocity can be a powerful tool for growing your influence. Done cynically, you will only succeed in undermining your credibility.

Questions to reflect on

1. How well do you know your stakeholders – peers, team members and those more senior than you? Do you know what they want and need? And is that insight up to date?

2. When you want to influence an outcome, how well is your argument underpinned by compelling evidence, presented in a way which meets your audience's needs rather than your own thought process?

3. How do you stay attuned to changing context within your organization in order to be able to pick your moment wisely?

Resources

Building reputation

Your actions, combined with what others say about you, create your reputation. This link contains ten tips to help you consider how you come across to others in person as well as online, written by Darrah Brustein for *Forbes* online, www.forbes.com/sites/yec/2014/01/28/10-simple-ways-to-improve-your-reputation

Stakeholder management

Being able to identify and prioritize stakeholders is critical to knowing your audience. The following steps in stakeholder identification and analysis techniques have been defined in a resource created by the Chartered Management Institute (CMI). The CMI has a very wide range of resources, many of which you can access simply by registering free of charge as a 'Friend'. Once you have done this, you can download the guide which provides the detail for each of the steps below, www.managers.org.uk/knowledge-and-insights/resource/stakeholder-analysis-and-management

Nine steps to identify and analyse stakeholders:

1. Gather information
2. Identify stakeholder groups
3. Map your stakeholders
4. Be specific
5. Prioritize your stakeholders
6. Understand your stakeholders
7. Develop strategies for action
8. Communicate and develop relationships with stakeholders
9. Monitor and review

Speaking truth to power

'Speaking truth to power' is a commonly used phrase, especially in the public sector. As Megan Reitz says, 'most leaders are blind to just how difficult it is for others to speak up to them.' This applies to managers as well as leaders. Her article in *HR Magazine*, written with John Higgins, can be found at www.hrmagazine.co.uk/article-details/the-difficulties-of-speaking-truth-to-power.

Reitz has videos on her website www.meganreitz.com/speakup covering a range of topics from her book *Speak up*, written with John Higgins, such as knowing the risks, understanding power and politics and listening effectively to others.

Notes

[1] Henry Timms and Jeremy Heimans, *New power* (Macmillan, 2018), p. 18.

[2] Roger Fisher and William Ury, *Getting to yes* (Random House, 2012).

[3] Quote attributed to Wilson Mizner during a radio interview in 1932, https://quoteinvestigator.com/2010/10/16/be-nice-on-way-up [accessed 15 December 2020].

4 Implementing change

Why it matters

Managing change is not only an increasingly frequent part of a manager's role, but is essential in the modern world of work. Almost every interaction we have can be connected back to creating change in one way or another. So being adept at this is now a core skill for any manager. This is not about the programmatic processes and tools (important and useful though they can be). This is about the single biggest determinant of successful change – bringing people on that journey. Doing this well accelerates performance and realizes the full potential of the change.

This chapter will take you through the why, what and how in change, including how you change behaviours.

Managers have lots of experience about the past: some of it is relevant to the future and some is not.

Manager, public sector

Understanding the *why*

If you've not experienced organizational change, or been involved in shaping and delivering it to one extent or another, then you are a rarity! In an increasingly volatile world, the only certainty we can rely on is that things will change. We now have a device in our pockets that has the same computing power as that which put a man on the moon 50 years ago. We can communicate visually with anyone around the world at a touch of a button, whereas when we started work around 30 years ago we would dictate our missives and send them to a typing pool, then they would reach our intended recipient some days later. The pace of change has been relentless and it's only getting faster.

But despite this, change is an uncomfortable prospect for many people. It creates risk and insecurity and that triggers an instinct to resist. This is a perfectly normal reaction. Change as a process to achieve a well-supported goal will always be better received than change which is imposed and unwelcome, with the impact on people's personal life often overlooked. It's important that you understand the rationale, but it is as important that you try to understand it from the perspective of the recipient. This table is a helpful prompt for your reflection on how change might be perceived.

Intentional change	Imposed change
Anticipated	Unexpected
Considered	Arbitrary
Timely	Creates problems
Solves problems	Disrupts process and routines
Provides new opportunities	Affects personal life

Whatever the reason for the change, having a compelling *why* narrative which sets out the vision for the change is vital framing. You need to be able to articulate why changes are being made and the improved outcomes this will realize. A tendency towards action often causes people to dive straight into the *what* without fully explaining the *why*. Ensuring people understand what's in it for them, as well as the organization, will increase motivation and support.

But the reality of perpetual change is that it leads to fear and people become passive or disengaged. Transparency and trust are preconditions, and that means being open about the vision the change will realize. It creates the foundation for an open dialogue.

The *how* trumps the *what* in successful change

There are plenty of well-rehearsed models out there for how to manage change based on how people respond. But there is less on how you actually implement change in a way to minimize its negative impact, and increase its adoption. And the big learning here is that it has absolutely nothing to do with *what* you are changing, it is resolutely and unremittingly about *how* you choose to go about it.

Case study: A reference point for this claim

I've delivered hundreds of changes in dozens of organizations. From incremental continuous improvements, through to highly complex transformations, the principles are consistent. And very rarely applied. The thing that's being changed – a new operating model, new technology, new process – is where the energy goes. Designing the *what*, shaping the future state, building a plan as to what the gap is between the current and desired future. Then with a need to see results, the energy gets channelled into executing the plan – making structural changes, installing or building new technology, designing processes. And when that work starts, resistance is encountered, progress slows and there's that dawning realization that in the focus on the *what*, the *how* has been forgotten. The *how* is what makes change stick. The *how* is where outcomes are achieved and benefits realized. And the *how* is about changing people's behaviour.

Now I understand why organizations always get this the wrong way round. The decision to make a change, thinking about what it might be, designing it and planning for it has taken time. They've got a clearly defined end goal and just want to get there, and all the associated benefits, as quickly as they can. It's counterintuitive to stop at that point, understand the impact of that change, and invest in more resource to actively mitigate that impact and support the behavioural change required for adoption. That just looks like a bunch of cost and delay. But without a shadow of a doubt, whatever the quantum of that cost and time is, it will be repaid many times over with a truly successful implementation. What comes next will be executed smoother and faster as a result, regaining all, if not more, of that time.

So if you take one thing away from how to implement change, it should be this: if you don't focus on changing people's behaviour, you'll never implement truly sustainable change. It's all about building a consensus and a commitment to that change. It's about leading and supporting the transitions that people need to make. It's about investing in those activities to accelerate outcomes.

> ### Case study: Proof that the *how* trumps the *what*
>
> A large NHS Trust had decided to invest in moving to an Electronic Patient Record. The case for change had been well evidenced and articulated: improved patient experience, better quality of care, reduced errors, better infection control arrangements, all of which led to a significant positive financial impact, as well as the experiential and qualitative improvements. The procurement for the technology had been done in a way that engaged senior clinicians and nursing staff who would have to use the system. The process design to configure the system for various specialities was done with great rigour.
>
> But as it was rolled out, the project team reported seeing those using the system still walking around with pen and paper. No effort had gone into identifying, and then supporting, the behavioural change required. Instead there was an assumption that as the end users had been engaged in choosing the system, they would just start using it as soon as the training came. The reality was that they simply subverted the new system to maintain the status quo.

Changing behaviours

Before we get into the five simple steps for the effective implementation of change, we're going to start from the assumption that the change you are implementing has been properly thought through. Appropriate thinking has gone into why it needs to happen and what you hope to achieve. Lessons have been learned from past organizational and individual experience. Evidence has been used to inform decision-making. You know what the change looks like and you understand the gap between the current and future states. Now, *before* you start planning for delivery, take the following steps – all of which are done in conjunction with people, engaging them at every step on the way.

1. Understand the impact of the change
    Take a methodical approach to mapping the groups of people who would be impacted by the change. It might be specific functional areas, departments or teams. It could just be single individuals. But look at that gap analysis and plot all those affected and why. Keep it high level at this stage, for example:

    *   Is there a process or policy change they'll need to comply with?
    *   Is there a new way of working which will require practical training, whether that be processes or technology?
    *   Will the shape or number of job roles be impacted by this change?

    Map the constituencies against the type of change, plotting which will be affected by each element. Some will be impacted by all, e.g., a new operating model fundamentally changing a team structure and ways of working; some by one component, e.g., the way that customers or other departments interact with that area. Completing this task gives you your change impact assessment. Now you can see the scale of the behavioural change you need to support in order to get the outcomes you hope to achieve.

2. Define support measures
    You can define the type of intervention required to support those changes in broadly three categories: engagement, training or documentation. Every change impact you've identified will need engagement to win hearts and minds, underpinned by a comms plan and set pieces like workshops or other events; it will just be a question of degrees. If you want people to change their behaviour, you are going to need to provide specific input on any new skills or ways of working in some kind of formal training. And if you're to underpin the change with new standard operating procedures – in whatever form and level of detail your sector demands – then you're going to need some documentation. Every impact you have identified should have at least one intervention. Some will require more than one. Taking this methodical approach allows you to map everyone impacted against the intervention required to support them – no chance of anything falling between the cracks.

3. Design your change approach

Now you truly understand the change challenge ahead, you can consider how you want to approach it. Is there some logic to the way you would sequence that support? Are there groups of people who require more support earlier, later or throughout? Are there constraints on when and how you can offer that support, e.g., legal requirements for organizational restructures or redundancy programmes, or times to avoid due to business-as-usual pressure peaks? What interventions are transition critical, i.e., key to the successful deployment of whatever is being changed? And what interventions are benefit critical, i.e., key to encouraging adoption and sustaining that change after deployment?

However you choose to tackle this, there are three inputs that will ensure you succeed:

- Start from a position of empathy
  Identifying those affected by the change, and determining what kind of intervention will support them through it, isn't an abstract exercise. Behind that data and map are people who will either struggle to accept the change, or will be enthusiastic adopters, and every shade in between. There's a model to help you identify where people might be on that spectrum in the Resources section. Every recipient is a person who'll be looking at what you are changing through their lens, not yours. Everything you design should be done with your audience in mind: their needs, their convenience, their preferences. All complemented with a healthy dose of energy and pace to counteract the human preference to resist change.

- Honesty really is the best policy
  People aren't stupid. They'll have got an inkling of what's coming. Secrets are rarely kept in organizations. Myths will have abounded. Wrong ends of sticks firmly grasped. There'll also be times when you need to communicate with partial information or not be able to answer people's questions. The only way to be consistent and successful in your change approach is to be unfailingly honest and compassionate, recognizing that what is required for one group might not work for another. And that includes a willingness to make it OK to say

'I don't know', and signal when you might. Badly implemented change has overly corporate, paternalistic and, sometimes unwittingly, arrogant communication.

- Be creative, but be pragmatic
Every change is unique and your change approach will need to reflect this. Of course there'll be principles, learning and practice from the last time you did this well that you can build on. But change is not a case of one size fits all. Even when it looks comparable it isn't – two departmental restructures will be underpinned by two different *whys*, two different sets of prevailing context, two different sets of personalities. So you'll need to be creative to design interventions that are appropriate... but also proportionate. In a world where time is an increasingly precious commodity, and those impacted are often geographically dispersed, you need to be pragmatic about the most effective way in which your interventions can land. Based on their needs, not your desires.

4. Bake it into your plan
Now you have a change plan. One that is based on a firm foundation of the variable impact of the change on different audiences. Which has specified the kinds of interventions to mitigate that impact. Which has fed into an overall change approach that is appropriate, proportionate and empathetic to your audience. Now you can turn that into a delivery plan. You've got the *why*, *who* and *what*, now for the *when* and *where*. Timing is key. Are your interventions laying the groundwork for other activities in the delivery plan to land, are they happening at the same time or supporting after the event? Some will be all of these. The point is, you are baking the resources and time required to bring people on their change journey into your delivery plan up front, not as an afterthought.

5. Listen, learn and refine
No matter how brilliant you are, and how good your evidence base is for the plan, you'll learn from doing. As the old military saying goes: no plan ever survives contact with the enemy![1] Feedback is the engine room for refining and developing your plan as you implement it. Ask for feedback and act on it. Learn from the early stage results. Refine your plan. Hone and improve as you go.

If that all feels like a lot of work, we'd say two things. Investing the time to do this properly reaps rewards in the long run. And whatever time you do invest should be proportionate to the change you're seeking to implement. Those five steps might take five minutes, they might take five weeks. Well, maybe not five minutes, but you get the point. Proportionality is key. While that's flexible, the principles are not.

Questions to reflect on

1. When implementing change do you spend as much time thinking about the *how* as the *what?*

2. Are there adequate time and resources in your plans to bring people on the change journey?

3. How are you planning to support people after the change deployment to ensure change is sustained and benefits realized?

Resources

Creating a compelling reason, the *why*

Simon Sinek is probably best known for his TED talk on the concept of the *why* being critical to leaders. It has been viewed more than 50 million times and is the third most watched video on TED.com. It's incredibly powerful and if you want people to follow you, watch him explain why: www.ted.com/talks/ simon_sinek_how_great_leaders_inspire_action?language=en

Why change fails

There are so many models for implementing change and probably none more famous than Kotter's eight-step process for leading change www.kotterinc.com/8-steps-process-for-leading-change. However, the reality is that many change efforts don't deliver their intended results so it can really help to identify and avoid the pitfalls. Dr Peter Fuda's thought-provoking analysis of why change efforts fail and what can be done to increase the likelihood of success can be found via this link, www. yumpu.com/en/document/view/24559957/why-change-efforts-fail

Change curve for individuals, teams and organizations

This is often called the SARAH model (based on Dr Elisabeth Kübler-Ross[2]) and describes the stages that people go through when they have a shock, which is often associated with change. This can help you to predict people's responses so you know what will help them get to acceptance. Moving through the stages can be slow or fast, people dip in and out and sometimes get stuck: remember the stages apply to you too.

- **S**hock
- **A**nger
- **R**esistance/denial
- **A**cceptance
- **H**ope/commitment

Leadership specialists Insights provide a good guide to the change curve and there is a free guide to coaching people through change available through this link, www.insights.com/resources/coaching-people-through-the-change-curve

Notes

[1] Quote attributed to Helmuth von Moltke (1800–91), www.oxford reference.com/view/10.1093/acref/9780191826719.001.0001/q-oro-ed4-00007547 [accessed 15 December 2020].

[2] *Elisabeth Kübler-Ross model on the five stages of grief,* www.ekrfoundation. org/elisabeth-kubler-ross [accessed 15 December 2020].

Part two
People

Because it's always about people

This section covers all things people-related. You and the core tenets of working with others. Because people are where the magic happens. We will take you through how you develop a people-centred approach to leading and managing teams, how you get the best out of others, have difficult conversations well and make meetings as effective as possible.

Putting people at the heart of the strategy, it's all about people and bringing everyone together. For me, the most powerful thing an organization has is the assets in people's heads. Trying to get all their tacit knowledge and make it explicit, getting it shared, which raises the capability of the organization on how to do certain things.

Manager, private sector

5 Managing authentically

Why it matters

You can only be people-centred if first you understand yourself. Knowing what drives you enables you to operate authentically and fulfil your potential with ease. It enables you to be the best version of yourself. It ensures that you get the best out of your team. It starts with knowing yourself and is accelerated by having a growth mindset.

This chapter is all about you – how to find your own authentic voice, develop your self-awareness and how to take care of yourself on your own journey.

Authenticity

We have our own values and belief systems – the things that guide us, our moral compass, our north star, the things which going against would seem to compromise our integrity.

Our values and our personality drive our behaviours and how they manifest themselves from day to day. Our attitude. Our moods. Our response to any given situation. They are visible to others in how we operate. Risk-averse or risk-taker. Shy or confident. Procrastinator or completer-finisher.

And we all require different stimuli to nourish those different parts of us. Our social life, family, exercise, hobbies, culture and our work.

Work is personal to you too. It could be a means to an end, it could be your vocation. It could align to your values in a way which gives you purpose. It could be about pushing your intellectual development. And these drivers may change over time.

Being authentic just means being yourself. And that is your whole self – what you believe in, your personality preferences, the way you behave, the things that matter to you, your motivation. Yet, so many people don't bring their whole selves to work. They bring the part that they think they should show.

That judgement is formed by a whole host of external factors. The prevailing culture of the organization. The behaviour of your peers and manager. The desire to fit in. And ultimately, they impact on your confidence to be yourself.

So why bother? Why not just show the bits of you that you need to and keep the rest private?

We know it can sometimes be hard to bring your whole self to work. But pretending to be something that you're not, or hiding a part of you, is not good for your mental health and wellbeing. A life at work and then your life outside of work might sound like a sensible compartmentalizing strategy, but taken to extremes – where you deny who you are or feel constrained at being able to be yourself – is exhausting, debilitating and damaging.

Case study: Learning the importance of authenticity the hard way

My innate different facets are an extrovert, risk taking, fixing, completer-finisher who needs purpose in their work. I've been told I'm highly productive and my initial success was all derived from getting stuff done. I'd turn up, be resolutely task-focused, cross everything off my to-do list and then leave for the day.

A few weeks into a fixed-term contract in the marketing department of a large retailer, the marketing director asked to have a chat with me. Once the small talk was done he started asking me what I knew about my colleagues. As he reeled off each name I offered what I knew – where they lived, how many children, their pets and so on. After we'd done this for three or four colleagues he then posed the killer question: what would they say about you? I realized that they didn't know anything about me. I didn't do small talk. I didn't drink tea or coffee so no opportunities for casual kitchen chat. I came in, sat at my

---

desk, got stuff done, left. He pointed out the value of building a connection and a rapport with people and why it mattered. But on reflection, I'm not sure I really got it.

As I progressed through my career, I leaned more and more into those things that had brought me success – not unusual for any of us. When your approaches are rewarded with achievement they become habitual. My getting stuff done got more prodigious. The stuff I was fixing got more complex. I got more senior roles. And, unsurprisingly, developed that old school style of hero leadership. Exhorting people to follow me up the big hill. I was better at the small talk and with a good memory, could chat about family, pets, holidays and hobbies with team members when required. But I was still resolutely task-focused.

And while my work life was, to anyone looking in, a success story, my own value and self-worth had become completely tied up in my ability to get stuff done. To say I was task- rather than people-focused is too simplistic, especially as I'm a natural people person who builds rapport easily. But getting the tasks done was what drove my interaction with people. And the more I developed the work version of myself, the more it separated me from who I was as a person.

After 17 years of constantly pushing myself harder and harder I finally fell over. Breakdown. Mental health crisis. Whatever you want to call it, my body finally told my brain it was time to stop and made me sleep for six weeks solid before I started to take a look at the patterns in my life that I needed to change. This experience enabled me to truly understand what it meant to be authentic, and took me back to those wise words from my marketing director all those years ago.

If I'm honest I used to dismiss the rise of authenticity as just the latest management trend. People are who they are, simple, right? Then I realized that I hadn't been me at work, I had been the work me. I spent time understanding what drove me to work the way I did. To disaggregate the natural skills and abilities that I had, from what drove me to deploy them the way I did. It didn't mean I had to quit what I was good at, but I had to rethink how I did it.

I took the metaphoric underpants from outside my trousers and went to work as me. The whole me. The me that had doubts and didn't have all the answers. The me that had good days and bad. The me that had plenty to offer from my experience and expertise. In balance. I stopped feeling like when I took off the suit I switched from one person to another. And I understood what it was to be truly authentic.

The subsequent ten years or so of my working life have still contained prodigious productivity, fixing difficult problems and getting stuff done. But I've done it with humility and kindness, and always start with people rather than the problem. And empathy has become my guiding principle.

Authenticity is not just a buzzword, it's about being at peace with who you are. Every idiosyncrasy. Every brilliant talent. Every irritating weakness. Seeing the value in yourself and acknowledging how others value you, even if you find that hard to see. Authenticity is grounding. Calming. Accepting. It is open. It enhances your accessibility and approachability in the eyes of others. It is real. It is you. And there's a useful resource on this at the end of this chapter.

Self-awareness

One of the best things we've seen about understanding what drives authentic leadership was the presentation of a leadership framework for the 21st century which is relevant at any point in your career. It was produced by Within People and is based on research with global business leaders from all sectors. It posited that there are eight fundamental qualities required for leadership in the modern world of work.

The framework was developed further to explore what it is that holds us back from fully realizing those qualities – what was it we had to unlearn in order to unleash? We've included the framework and the exercise for you to work through in the Resources section – understanding what drives you and unleashing your full potential is key to ensuring you are an authentic and empathetic leader and manager.

Knowing yourself helps you to have the self-awareness and compassion to see things from another perspective. The drawing of the old/young woman below reminds us that people can look at the same thing and see it differently. There's no right or wrong, just a difference in perspective – something that is easy to forget when the pressure is on.

Optical illusion

© Granger Historical Picture Archive / Alamy Stock Photo

Case study: The value of understanding others as well as yourself

While working for a FTSE 100 company, I was leading a project to launch three new websites which was falling behind schedule. My reflections from a team meeting that had not gone well made me realize there was a general lack of commitment and frustrations were causing blame. I recognized that despite the team members being highly skilled, the dynamic between them was not good.

I tentatively made this observation at the next meeting and asked if people would be willing to have an individual team profile done on the understanding that this would be shared with the whole team. I was surprised and relieved when everyone agreed. That in itself was a useful reminder that everyone really did want the project to succeed.

A facilitator supported us throughout the process of interpreting our profiles in the individual reports and sharing our personal preferences with other team members. The results highlighted that each of us had different approaches to the work, from detail conscious to big picture vision.

The results were transformative. It allowed the programmers to tell me that there would be no customer experience if the coding didn't work, and for me to remind them of what the company was trying to achieve for the customer and why. This conversation could take place because we understood that we each bought different skills to the project, so issues were discussed openly and without irritation.

To this day, I am acutely aware that my preference is for conceptual thinking and I'm always grateful for those who are good with detail.

Our personality traits become ingrained in childhood and are at the root of how we react to situations. Everyone has them and understanding your own helps you to understand others and to be empathetic to their needs. They underpin your motivation, leadership approach, communication style, decision-making and how you judge others – including stereotyping. They also influence how you manage disagreement and stress.

On a practical level, if you haven't yet done any kind of psychometric assessment, it's worth looking at the tools available to you to better understand your own personality traits (MBTI[1] and FIRO-B[2]) and when your strengths can become weaknesses, as in the Hogan Development Survey.[3] They often provide you with insight which will help you better understand other people's reactions too.

Sports psychologist Dr Steve Peters described why people behave irrationally in his book *The chimp paradox*.[4] He describes how the limbic system, as the more primitive and immediate part of our brain, acts on feelings and emotions; it can override the rational part of our brain in the frontal lobe. This limbic system is evolutionarily much older, designed to protect us from harm, hence why it is triggered faster than the logical element. He defines this as our 'inner chimp', which can take over and cause us to react irrationally.

The subconscious mind is programmed to answer the questions we ask and bring up supporting evidence. That's why reflection in a negative frame of mind will bring up unhelpful evidence, whereas asking yourself about what you've learnt will bring up a very different response from your subconscious. For example compare 'why do all my projects fail?' to 'how does this event help me to achieve my aim?'

As well as understanding yourself and others being a key tenet of operating authentically, this also has practical advantages as we work in ways where we are no longer expected to have all the answers. Collaborating and tapping into the ideas of others necessitates the ability to understand other people's styles and build rapport effectively. This emotional intelligence – or emotional capability as it is better described – is critical to developing empathy and authenticity.

When you have a clear understanding of yourself then you can assess whether the role and organization you work for are aligned with your values and preferences. If they are not aligned, you can survive for a while but not thrive. Behaving in a way that is at odds with your normal self becomes exhausting and leads to stress and possibly burnout.

Being grounded by your authentic self, informed by self-awareness, means that you have control of yourself and your reactions.

Self-care

There is often not much help around and people aren't admitting they need it even if they do. There might be a lot of fear admitting that you're under pressure, you're anxious about things... there are all these swirling emotions which you get and you can feel like there aren't networks or support mechanisms readily at hand. Unless you have really good friends or a mentor to discuss it with, it can be hard to deal with.

Manager, private sector

We all know that our own wellbeing is essential to our ability to perform well. And that we have a responsibility to do this for our teams. In that order – think of the airline reminder to put our own oxygen mask on before helping others. So why do we neglect this most important of priorities?

Thankfully, the culture of presenteeism and the long hours associated with it are in decline, but that doesn't mean that the work–life balance challenges have gone away. Quite the opposite. Technology means we are always on. The predominance of home-working for those who used to be in offices as a result of coronavirus mean those boundaries are more blurred than ever. There is plenty of research that tells us that the increasing time we spend at work has a negative impact on productivity, as well as a decline in the ability to problem-solve. Innovation and creativity dries up and, worst of all, we drain our reserves so there is nothing to draw on when there is an urgent need for us to respond.

There are countless ways in which we can all find our own peace with the modern world of work. And even more resources out there to support you in this. What is vital is that you do whatever it is that works for you to take care of your physical and mental wellbeing. Doing this is what generates your resilience. And for the avoidance of doubt, we do not believe for a moment that resilience is about toughening up or being able to withstand more pressure or stress than you used to be able to. Quite the opposite. Resilience is about how you optimize your performance. It is not a static state. Resilience will change in response to your experience. Whether you've had a great day or you are wrestling with an intractable problem, the important point is to recognize how you are feeing and take measures to ensure you can cope. That is true resilience – having agency over your own wellbeing. There's a great resource for assessing your resilience at the end of this chapter.

A good starting point is to think about your response to setbacks, which we covered in more detail in Chapter 2. Do you tend to look for what went well and the learning you've generated for the future or do you dwell on the negatives? Reflection is essential for learning, but negative naval gazing can be destructive in the longer term. Do you measure your success relative to your own experience and career journey or do you compare yourself to others? Relative comparisons can often create further hurdles in your mind and rarely leads to a sense of fulfilment, whereas recognizing how much valuable experience you have gained compared to where you were six months, a year or three years ago is a much more meaningful assessment.

Our top three tips for self-care are simple. We know they're often cited, but they work, and there is more signposting to resources on all of these at the end of this section.

1. Sleep: so often overlooked, this is the basic building block for everyone's wellbeing and is one of the most performance-enhancing things you can focus on. There is plenty of evidence that continued sleep deprivation impairs judgement, decision-making and your ability to perform. There is a reason why sleep deprivation is used as a form of torture!

2. Mindfulness: this has long been accepted as a driver of improved performance at work. The ability to switch your mind off is critical to your wellbeing. The tumble dryer effect of continually churning over problems drains energy and creates a negative mindset. It crowds your mind with white noise which prevents those 'aha' moments that often occur at unexpected times. If you think about when you last had one of those moments, we bet it wasn't when you were sat at your desk dealing with emails! Building mindfulness or meditation practice into your routine is an excellent self-care choice.

3. Manage distractions: we're so used to having at least one mobile device next to us at any one time that it's almost become an

extension of our anatomy! The constant ping of notifications is designed to be irresistible and generate a response. Finding a balance between being connected to the things that you want and need to be connected to, and space where they don't prevent you being fully present in other activities helps maintain calm and concentration. Consider switching off non-urgent notifications and using silent mode.

Questions for reflection

1. What drives you at work? Does that come from a good place that makes you connect with who you are?

2. Do you bring your whole self to work? If you are hiding any part of you, why is that?

3. Looking at the Within People framework in the Resources section, what is it that you need to unlearn to unleash your potential?

4. Do you prioritize your own wellbeing? If not, how can you take better care of yourself?

Resources

Framework for authentic leadership

The Within People framework has identified eight qualities that their research says are essential for effective leadership for the 21st century.

Look at this list and choose the one that you think that has served you best in your working life to date:

Vulnerability
Creativity
Courage
Conviction
Empathy
Curiosity
Patience
Love

It can be really hard to choose just one, but once you've picked that quality, take a few moments to really reflect on why you chose it. What is it about that quality that has served you well and why?

Now think about the quality that you struggle with the most. This tends to be an easier choice than the first one.

Again, once you've chosen it, take a few moments to reflect on what it is that gets in the way of you deploying that quality more frequently.

What can you do to change that? Be purposeful about what you're going to do differently at work in order to make that not the case in the future.

And finally, turn over to see the things that we all need to unlearn, in order to unleash the innate potential of each of those leadership qualities.

QUALITY ➡	UNLEARN ➡	UNLEASH
Vulnerability	Shame	Authenticity
Creativity	Failure	Freedom
Courage	Smallness	Power
Conviction	Self-doubt	Vision
Empathy	Solving	Connection
Curiosity	Prejudice	Learning
Patience	Doing	Presence
Love	Separation	Heart and soul

© Within People. Reproduced with permission www.withinpeople.com

Authenticity

Associate Professor Natalia Karelaia at INSEAD writes about what it means to be your authentic self at work and the advantages it can bring. You can access it here, https://knowledge.insead.edu/leadership-organizations/the-advantages-of-being-seen-as-authentic-14741

Assessing your own resilience

Roffey Park Institute has a questionnaire to help you assess how resilient you are across five domain areas:

- perspective
- purpose, values and strengths

- emotional intelligence
- physical energy
- connections

The Resilience Capability Index takes 5–10 minutes to complete and at the end you will have a score, which is compared with a relevant norm group. You can access it via this link, www.roffeypark.ac.uk/knowledge-and-learning-resources-hub/resilience-capability-index

Self-care online resources

Sleep apps:

- Pzizz
- Sleepio
- Sleepstation (requires a GP referral)

Mindfulness apps:

- Headspace
- Calm

Mindfulness: there's a wealth of resources on Mindful.org

Notes

[1] *Myers-Briggs Type Indicator (MBTI) personality inventory*, www.myersbriggs.org/my-mbti-personality-type/mbti-basics [accessed 15 December 2020].

[2] *FIRO B workplace relations*, https://eu.themyersbriggs.com/en/tools/FIRO [accessed 15 December 2020].

[3] *Hogan Development Survey*, www.hoganassessments.com/assessment/hogan-development-survey [accessed 15 December 2020].

[4] Steve Peters, *The chimp paradox* (Vermilion, 2012).

6 Getting the best out of others

Why it matters

Managing teams means you have responsibility to create an environment where everyone can be the best version of themselves. If you get the best out of your people, everybody wins. The bedrock of these relationships is trust – a rare commodity in the modern world, making it even more valuable in the workplace. Getting the best out of your people should be the priority for every manager. Not only will it enable you to retain, develop and grow your team, it will deliver great performance along the way.

This chapter will start with your boss, before moving on to your team and the importance of trust in all interactions with others.

Let's start with your boss

When you think about the topics we've covered already – the ability to put yourself in other's shoes, see things from their perspective, frame your needs through their lens – they all have empathy at their core. And building a relationship with your boss that is mutually beneficial, and allows you to be the best version of yourself at work, requires empathy and authenticity too.

It's very common when we start a new job for others to ask questions of you, whether it's one-to-one induction meetings, your first team meeting or other settings. You'll be invited to share a bit about who you are and your background in one way or another. Your introduction to the organization and those you'll be working with. We're making this observation here as we can't help but wonder how often you did the same with your boss – either when you started or once you were settled in? Very often, status, hierarchy or nerves when you're in a new job prevent you from doing this.

Taking the time out to ask about others is an important core skill, not just to be empathetic, but to gain insight as to the best way to work together. Asking open, curious questions of your boss is a rich source of learning. Asking about their experience and how they got where they are will give you insight for your own journey. Asking about why they chose to work in this organization will give you insight as to their motivation. Asking about what they see as the key risks and opportunities will give you insight into potential pitfalls and how you might be able to add value. Asking about what success looks like – for them and for you in your role – gives you the anchor point for objective setting and your own development needs. You get so much rich material from just a few open questions.

And of course, this works both ways. Understanding your boss is half of the equation, to work together optimally, they need to understand you too. If they don't naturally ask the same of you, then you might need to share it with them as part of that conversation. And it needs to be honest. Authentic. If you're feeling nervous or daunted, say so. Give them a sense of your humility, as well as your enthusiasm and your talent. Be open about what it is you need support with, or what you're looking forward to learning about.

This kind of human, empathetic, authentic conversation builds a relationship that's based on mutual understanding. Its openness is the foundation of the trust dynamic between you both. It starts to develop a relationship that is a shared endeavour. It creates the conditions you'll need for them to get the best out of you, and for you to support their objectives too. Give it a try, you'll be surprised how impactful this can be.

It should also lay the groundwork for how you'll learn. We never stop learning, however expert we get. Even when our technical skills become finely honed, the context and environments in which they are deployed vary, the personalities and situations you encounter are new. Learning abounds every day. Organizational culture is a big determinant in how learning is obtained. An agile, scaling start-up may have a 'fail fast' mentality where they crave mistakes to inform the next iteration. A large corporate may find that an anathema and, perhaps unwittingly, create an environment of blame or fear of admitting mistakes. And there'll be every shade in-between.

Having an open conversation with your boss about the ways and opportunities for learning, and your own personal growth, will help frame the best approach to this. It also lays the foundation to explore that learning with someone else and get the value of their experience on your journey. People like to be asked for help and to share their expertise – tapping into that will further strengthen your relationship and help them get the best out of you.

And finally, if it's done with sufficient empathy and humility, it should also allow you to bring your whole self into the conversation. What are your red flags, constraints or requirements for a good work–life balance? It might be that you struggle if you haven't had a good night's sleep or sufficient time for regular exercise. Share this with the people you work with and for. It helps create an unspoken narrative where you understand each other with a shorthand. It also moves you away from the old style hero mode where it's all about being resilient. Pushing yourself and your resilience isn't healthy. Maintaining a connection with who you are, what you need, and having some agency over managing that is much easier to do when you've been open about this with your boss.

There are plenty of practical things that you can then do – regular meetings, embedding feedback in your work together, establishing clear requirements and expectations. And remembering that saying no, prioritizing and managing your own capacity is all part of these ongoing discussions. All of these are great tactical tools. But without a relationship built on empathy and trust they'll only ever be superficial and you won't help your boss get the best out of you.

Trust as the glue

Before we get into what we think good team working looks like, let's tackle the issue of trust. Without trust, no relationship can survive, let alone thrive. Mistrust leads to suspicion and erroneous assumptions. Both of these can quickly shape an individual's perception as their own reality, which becomes impossible to break down.

We're both the kind of people whose instinct is to trust first and only revise that position if someone does something to lose our trust. If you are the same, it is easy to believe that others think as you do. Only when you encounter less trusting individuals can you truly understand the corrosive nature that an absence of trust creates, and how completely it undermines your ability to get the best out of others, and yourself.

Case study: The consequences of an absence of trust

I'd joined a new organization with a small team of six direct reports who were all remotely based. Everyone across that team was very experienced in their fields. I also had broader leadership responsibilities across the organization, as well as ambassadorial duties representing us externally.

I started out, as I usually do, getting to know the team members. With two or three people there was a good instant connection, but the majority of the conversations were hard in terms of building rapport or being able to establish my own credibility and authenticity with them. I didn't connect with them at a level of shared values or purpose. I was a very different personality to most of them. I came away from those sessions with the overriding sense that this was going to be a challenging set of people.

What followed was a series of now obvious, but understandable, mistakes.

First, I didn't make the investment of additional time with them individually or as a group to try and overcome the initial barriers to building trust and confidence. My conscious justification for this was based around the breadth of my responsibilities and limitations on my time, combined with their general lack of availability. Subconsciously, I was no doubt avoiding putting myself in a situation that may have led to difficult conversations with individuals I felt were quite challenging.

Second, I relied on the strengths of the results in the other areas of my responsibilities to have some kind of radiated impact on their perception of me. It's a classic human response to lean in to your strengths and, in some cases, overplay them, as a compensatory mechanism. The other two areas of my responsibilities were being delivered exceptionally well, with resoundingly positive feedback. I used that as a positive reinforcing mechanism around my strengths, rather than tackling the weakness in my performance regarding these relationships.

Third, I didn't factor in the impact of their shared history versus me being a new arrival. They may have been a remote team who physically came together rarely, but half of them had worked together for seven years, the other half for between two and four years. They'd been leaderless for the best part of a year and had established their own ways of working, underpinned by their own, varying, levels of trust in each other. And I was new.

By not investing sufficient time to break through any barriers to building trust, none was created.

The remote nature of the team meant that the positive feedback I was receiving in other areas of my work, that may have provided some credibility to support the nurturing of trust, wasn't visible to them.

And despite the red flag in an early team meeting regarding the approach they took to trust being opposite to mine – they started from a position of zero trust and people had to earn it – I didn't modify my approach. Instead I tried to challenge the illogical nature of their approach, rather than empathetically putting myself in their shoes and changing my tactics to build rapport.

The longer the failure to establish trust continued, the more relationships deteriorated. Every idea or suggestion from me was challenged or ignored. Whether it was simple administrative matters such as changing meeting dates through to more significant strategic or developmental activities.

Communication was already challenging, but as the resistance intensified, the relationships went beyond neutral to negative. It was only after they'd broken down to the point that I walked away from the role that I truly understood the corrosive nature of the lack of trust on every aspect of our relationship.

Without sufficient investment up front in establishing rapport, there'd been no effective lines of communication. As a result, simple acts of clarification and explanation were absent, which led to erroneous assumptions having a significant undermining impact.

For example, I wanted to observe some of the set piece activities across the team in the first few weeks. Keen not to change the dynamic of what I was seeing (while accepting that the very act of observing things change them), I would sit to one side. As a digital first, paper-free operator, I would rely on my iPad or phone to take notes. Whereas the team assumed that this meant I was disinterested and disengaged.

Another example related to the way I managed my email inbox. I'm an inbox zero junkie, and would always reply promptly whenever I was at my desk. As a significant proportion of my time was spent at events and external facing activities, I'd put a modified out of office reply on saying that I had intermittent access to emails and inviting people to contact me on my mobile if they needed a reply that day. Team members getting frequent out of office replies assumed that I wasn't putting the time in required for the role.

These are just two small, but powerful, examples of the psychological issues that a lack of trust have on the way we work together. On one hand, if I'd invested the additional time up front to establish my ways of working or approach with the team, who I could sense were innately challenging and distrustful, maybe I would at least have created an open line of communication where I could choose to explain or frame my actions to provide reassurance.

On the other hand, their instinctive choice not to trust and to always think the worst might have led them to a conclusion they wanted to believe, regardless of what I did. While they undoubtedly needed to be more generous, as their team leader it was down to me to build the necessary trust and confidence for us to operate effectively together.

Instead, the relationship slowly broke down entirely to the point where the differences were irreconcilable. While there is lots of learning as to why things went wrong in this example, the biggest lesson is this: if trust isn't built early, or issues regarding a lack of trust aren't tackled head-on in the initial phases of any new working relationship, they're unlikely to be recovered at a later stage. Without the foundation of trust, any attempts that I made to deploy the usual good practice to optimize team working were doomed to failure.

Trust in traditional institutions has been steadily declining over the past 20 years. The 2020 report by Edelman that has been tracking this shows that 'people today grant their trust based on two distinct attributes: competence (delivering on promises) and ethical behaviour (doing the right thing and working to improve society).'[1] It is important for you to recognize that broad context you are working in and the expectations this will create in your team.

When we talk about building trust, we're not talking about blind faith. A bit of healthy cynicism and scepticism is always good. It creates productive tension and, when deployed effectively, a challenge that adds value and improves outcomes by offering a different point of view. We're talking about the fundamental definition of trust – a firm belief in the reliability, truth or ability of someone or something.

In order to do that, the person (or people) you're seeking to create trust with need to know something about you. Enough to give them a sense of who you are and why they should place that belief in you. Demonstrating your authenticity is crucial to this. And there's no shortcut to investing the time required to get to know those who you need to trust and want to trust you in return. These kinds of conversations only work if you're genuinely interested and engaged in what you hear – you can't fake that and people see it if you do. Authenticity builds trust and an initial investment in that relationship is crucial.

The research that Lucy Adams[2] did in the BBC during the notorious Savile crisis revealed that there were five simple behaviours that inspired trust:

- They know my name
- Their doors are always open
- They ask my opinion
- They remember what's going on in my life
- They acknowledge when they've got something wrong.

The relationship between trust, safety and belonging

Think about a time when you have been working in a team and have been able to give your best. The chances are that you have felt confident in yourself and trusted by your colleagues and manager to do a good job. The need to feel safe and without fear is a basic requirement of performance. If a team member is fearful of criticism or making a mistake, they will never work to the best of their capability.

The need for safety and belonging is one of the most frequently occurring themes in recent research. Having studied what makes for an ideal team for two years, Google identified five key characteristics, the first of which was psychological safety.[3] This was described as being able to take risks in the team without feeling insecure or embarrassed. There's a signpost to more reading on this at the end of the chapter. Daniel Coyle spent years researching the world's most successful groups, from which he identified three skills that tap into our programming as social beings.[4] These are built from the bottom up, as follows:

- Safety – where people feel confident they belong and can be themselves.
- Vulnerability – sharing concerns and admitting mistakes which builds trust.
- Purpose – decided by the team and which goes beyond an output or deliverable.

Belonging means a legitimate right to be part of a team and to be heard in an environment where it is safe to speak openly and without fear. Without security, people can't be adventurous and for this to happen, the manager has to remove threats, treating people as valued, and ensuring they have an equal opportunity to be heard.

Imagine yourself and think about how you feel in teams where you are a member rather than the leader. Can you share concerns in a safe environment where you will not be criticized or blamed, particularly if you're asking for help? If not, what would need to happen to make it safe? It is important to set boundaries on what behaviours are acceptable and what aren't.

Reflect on what makes you feel trusted by managers and peers and also what doesn't. Chances are that you feel confident to raise concerns and contrary opinions and that your boss will receive these in a calm and interested manner. Trust is an attribute and a value, something that can't always be won easily or quickly.

Once you've established the foundations of trust, you then need to continue to be your authentic self. Communicate openly and transparently, in the way you've started. Be curious. Don't pretend that you have all the answers.

My manager supports me and my team say I support them, which is nice. You never really master management because there's always something that changes.

Manager, public sector

Sharing vulnerability is a powerful way to build trust. In Brené Brown's *Dare to lead*, she identified that we derive strength from interdependence, not from individualism.[5] There's a signpost to more from Brown at the end of the chapter. She shows that adults seek to become someone whom others can depend on, rather than being autonomous and solitary. Using data collected over 20 years, she explores vulnerability as the basis of courage, which we now need more than ever in dealing with uncertainty and risk. Examples of sharing vulnerability as a manager might be admitting you don't know the answer. Saying you need the team's help is likely to be liberating for the team, creating the opportunity to make their own decisions when appropriate.

Engage with those you want to trust frequently and honestly. And watch out for the two biggest drivers of trust.

1. Investing time
   Some relationships will find that rapport in your first engagement. A meeting of minds, a connection over your authentic selves. We've all had these kinds of encounters. You feel like you've met a kindred spirit, hit it off instantly. That's brilliant. But with the many and varied spectrum of human life not every initial engagement will leave you feeling like that. Wariness, uncertainty,

challenge, difference – all of these are emotions that some encounters will leave you with. It's vital to recognize this. For the purposes of establishing trust, the important thing to notice is that this relationship, for whatever reason, is going to take more time. You can't get the foundations in place instantly with everyone. There's a great TED talk from Margaret Heffernan on this in the Resources section at the end of this chapter.

2. Your actions

    The most impactful thing you can do to create trust in the eyes of others is to always do what you say you will. Actions most definitely speak louder than words. The simple truth is that this is the single biggest tool you have to both build and erode trust. Each time you do it, it adds to the bank incrementally as you build and deepen trust over time. But it can be lost in a heartbeat with just one example of that not being the case.

Creating a high-performing team

The bedrock of effective team working is trust. Getting the best out of your team is only possible when trust is present, so everything we talk about in this section is based on the premise that the trust foundations are in place.

After that, getting the best out of your team is fundamentally about six things:

- Knowing your people
- Creating purpose
- Shaping culture
- Developing capability
- Valuing difference
- Capacity planning

1. Knowing your people

    You can't build trust or get your team working optimally without really getting to know them. When you join a new organization or team, looking at the labels of job titles or organizational structures automatically limits your understanding of the capability and capacity of your colleagues as they are only based on that moment in time. Instead, schedule 45 minutes with every team member, one-to-one, regardless of team size. Position these meetings openly as you just wanting to get to know them better. Have one fixed, but very open, question: tell me about yourself, give me your potted history. Encourage people to share their stories. Listen, engage and explore their journey with them. These kinds of conversations only work if you are genuinely interested and engaged in what you hear – you can't fake that and people see it if you do.

One of the great benefits of this kind of approach is it gives you a rounded set of information which spans the past, present and future. You understand an individual's journey and what brought them to that point. This gives you insight into their broader experience and capability beyond the job they have right now. You know what motivated them to take up their current role, and gain insight into what drives them and what success looks like for them. You get a sense of their future plans and how what they are doing now, and the experiences you are able to give them, will influence their ability for these aspirations to become reality.

This is invaluable in how you choose to manage that individual, but also in how you build the dynamic of the team. You may be able to see or create connections that others don't. You can see synergies and difference, and how that might support the goals of the team and that individual. You know where the development opportunities might exist and how you can support team members in remaining motivated. You have the foundations for ensuring that you get the best from the sum of the parts available to you.

2. Creating purpose
    Everyone comes to work for a reason. And that reason underpins individual motivation. Some people are motivated to make as much money as possible, and that's a perfectly legitimate motivation. But more often than not, people are driven to work by their values and inherent interests. This is a valuable tool in optimizing team performance.

It's much easier to create a sense of purpose around a key task or activity in a team. It can be well defined, with clear boundaries and definition of what success looks like. It has a prescribed start and end point. Creating a sense of purpose and belonging for an entire team can be much harder, especially in business-as-usual rather than project-based work.

So whatever sized cog your team is in the machine, take some time to create a sense of purpose that transcends the day-to-day. Not only will it generate enthusiasm and enhance motivation, it will also create a sense of commitment that you can lean into when times get tough. A north star that helps you navigate your way through challenges or ambiguity. And be mindful of the distinction between purpose among team members too. They can be complementary or corrosive.

Case study: The power of purpose

You've probably heard the one about the stonemason working on part of a wall who said he was building a cathedral, or the floor cleaner at NASA saying they were putting a man on the moon. The reason you hear these old stories so often is because they go to the heart of how you create a sense of purpose for the team.

I ran a customer contact centre once – not the most inspiring work to generate purpose. Sure, you can talk about providing excellent service or being customer-centric, but that's still quite transactional. In this particular example, it was a team working on administering grant payments for early adopters of renewable heat technologies. They'd be fielding calls from people who'd either got stuck on the online process or dealing with meter readings, audit and documentary requirements. At face value, perhaps not the most exhilarating topics.

But the scheme was the first of its kind in England and it was hoped to be a significant contributor to the Government's (then) 2020 carbon reduction targets. We used this higher sense of purpose to create an induction programme for staff that talked about the importance of the sustainability agenda for the future of the planet. The role that this scheme was playing in delivering those objectives. And we held it in an eco-lodge that gave truly inspirational and experiential insight into the importance of this for our generation and those that follow.

This not only created a sense of purpose for the team, but also a healthy and grounded evangelism among them about what they were contributing to. There was an innate sense of belonging to something bigger. There was pride in their work. This enthusiasm was evident when they dealt with customers, who themselves were leading the way by being early adopters. It drove their desire to help customers succeed in a way that no customer service metric or net promoter score ever could.

3. Shaping culture

You know your people. And you have a sense of purpose. Well now you need a culture that is going to deliver against that purpose. Every manager creates the culture and sets the tone for their team, regardless of the overarching organizational culture. It could be a fast-paced, experimental culture. It could be a process-driven, structured culture. Your purpose will determine the culture you want and need. And, with due regard to the overarching culture of the organization which will always set the overall tone, you have the opportunity to create the right culture for your team to excel.

The culture of your team is the biggest differentiator for success. There's plenty of research out there about the impact of organizational culture on performance. At its simplest, if you have two sets of people with comparable skills and experience, the same resources to complete a task, the differentiator isn't what they have, it's how they choose to accomplish it. Culture is *the* accelerant of team performance.

The most effective cultures are those that are co-created and, therefore, owned by everyone in the team. An overt process of contracting among team members which asks the question: how do we want it to feel like to work in this team? Then commit to reinforcing this by holding each other to account for it, with a safe and supportive feedback culture. We've included a simple framework at the end of this chapter that you can use with your teams which both illustrates why culture matters and kick starts the co-creation process.

Whatever the prevailing organizational culture, our experience tells us that the most common cultural features of effective teams are consistently demonstrated as:

- Autonomy: an environment which encourages maximum autonomy by agreeing clear outcomes for tasks and activities and allowing individuals to shape their own route to delivering that. This means you avoid micromanaging how the task is completed, but are content that the outcome you have set is met, and remain curious about the learning that you gain from the approach taken.

- Learning: an environment which actively promotes learning and personal growth. This requires you to create the time and space to reflect on recent learning and insights from the work that the team are engaged in. This could be simple reflections and feedback at the end of each team session, more structured lessons learned approaches, or the simple act of a compassionate enquiry of how your direct report is learning and developing in one-to-one meetings. The important thing is to make this part of the way of working for you and your team.

- Diversity: an environment that creates diversity of thought, ideas and approaches. Actively seeking team members with different experiences, styles and preferences will provide you with the foundations for good creative tension. This will require you to resist the urge to hire in your own image and ensure that every voice is heard when they are available to you.

People enjoy being bigged up. A member of my team created a VR experience for a client and I made sure that he got the full kudos for it. The Japanese part of the firm was learning from us and others wanted to copy the idea and I made sure his name was all over it. When people do great work they get the recognition for it.

Manager, private sector

- Celebrating success: while terms and conditions can't be easily influenced, the most powerful reward is entirely in the gift of the manager – saying 'well done' or 'thank you' for a job well done. This has such a positive impact and is woefully underused.

Whether it's 'thank you' or 'well done', this should be a key tool in your managerial armoury. Keep thank you and well done cards in your drawer wherever you work and take the time to hand-write them to celebrate contributions of team members – a lost art in the technological world. If you prefer to use technology, a WhatsApp equivalent can have the same effect. High-performing teams give each other five positive comments to every piece of constructive criticism – how does that ratio compare in your team?[6]

Case study: The power of symbolic rewards

While leading a project to become more customer-orientated in a FTSE 100 company, a colleague was tasked with setting up a call centre. It was a large bureaucratic organization and one where managers had no control over salary or bonuses as they were all set centrally.

The manager knew he needed a different culture in order to deliver excellent customer service but not having any control over remuneration in a city with many competitor call centres was a challenge. He realized the answer lay in motivating people. He did this by working alongside teams every day, getting to know each individual as well as praising and giving feedback.

His observation and coaching resulted in an event every Friday afternoon when he awarded a Mars bar to an individual for exceptional effort that week. He made this into a fun event and it quickly became the highlight of the call centre's week.

Because he worked alongside the staff taking the time to understand their difficulties and getting to know them, he earned a high level of trust and respect. This combined with the fact that he was the boss of the whole operation made the Mars bar something that was truly prized.

Whenever I visited the call centre there was a great atmosphere and it was clear how motivated people were to perform well which was in stark contrast to other areas of the business. And the cost? A Mars bar.

Your leadership should be the manifestation of the culture you want and need in the team. This builds confidence and motivation. It is true that people don't tend to leave companies, they tend to leave their managers. The key point for you is to distinguish when leadership is required rather than management. Leadership is about setting direction through a vision, inspiring people to make that vision a reality, while management is about process and getting things done. Dispiritingly, teams are frequently over-managed and under-led. Remember, it is your role to create an environment where people can give of their best. You create the culture for your team by your actions.

4. Developing capability
    While there will also be a cadre of people at work who are content to keep operating at the level they are at – and every organization needs these – there are many others who are looking to learn from their work. And even those who aren't motivated to progress their careers will encounter learning from new situations doing the same thing.

    Actively creating opportunities for skill development, and achieving mastery among team members is a core part of an effective team culture. Daniel Pink[7] is clear that challenge and mastery – along with having autonomy and purpose – is what really motivates people. It should seek to play to the different strengths and capabilities across the team. Including those you want to develop for the future. Which you know about because you've got to know your people. It should look to deepen core capabilities that are essential for everyone to deliver your purpose, e.g., what amazing customer service looks like. It should value the experiential and on-the-job development as much as traditional training and courses.

    It should focus as much, if not more, on how people do their work rather than what they do. Once you have accomplished a technical discipline there's always more to learn about how you deploy it. And there'll be a set of behaviours about how the team wants to work, that it shaped when it defined its optimum culture, that will need supporting too. At the very minimum this should include the skills required to embed a culture of feedback and continuous improvement, not least because this enables everyone to tackle any issues that arise across the team quickly and appropriately. Taking time regularly to reflect as a team is important, so you can spot early warning signs of things going wrong.

5. Valuing difference
    If you're lucky enough to have been part of a team that is genuinely greater than the sum of its parts, you'll probably recognize that one of the key features is the ability to value difference and diversity of perspectives. This is always more valuable than single views and should be a clear mitigation of the risk of you, as team leader, hiring people in your own image.

    Creating positive conflict in your team is an essential ingredient to gaining the advantage of different views and perspectives. This kind of productive tension should be encouraged as part of the culture and way of working. Seeking people not only with different technical areas of expertise, but also different thinking styles and approaches that will shine a new light on tasks and challenges when working together. Homogeneous teams are more prone to error and can have disastrous consequences, as Matthew Syed describes in the events leading up to 9/11.[8]

As the leader of the team, you need to use the knowledge of your people, their preferences, strengths and weaknesses to facilitate the maximum contribution from everyone you manage. As you do this, signalling the value and reinforcing the cultural principles you agree will make this the norm.

We talk about being busy, but it's really about how people are best using their time. Are we prioritizing the right things or delegating enough? Or are we at capacity and just don't have the resources at the moment? Instead of being reactive and taking on whatever comes to us – we need to be clearer about our own capacity.

Manager, third sector

Ultimately, your performance is always a reflection of the performance of your people. We're often asked to suggest what we think is the key ingredient for organizational or team success. Is it about having a clear vision, budget, plan or resources? And our answer from experience of working in hundreds of organizations is quite simple – it's *always* about people. We've seen first-hand that you can have all of the required ingredients, but the wrong people, and you'll fail. We've also seen first-hand that you could have none of the required ingredients, but have the right people, with the right attitude and the right culture and magic can happen. Your role as leader of any team is simple – to create an environment where everyone who works for you can be the best version of themselves. If you do that, you'll create optimum team working which will serve you all well in good times and bad.

6. Capacity planning

Knowing your team and creating the right culture is vital. But you also have a role as their manager to ensure that you manage the capacity you have across your team. It allows you to objectively assess what time you have to allocate to priorities and, if it isn't enough, gives you an evidence base for why you need more resources or to stop doing something.

Our team away-day produced a list of issues, what they could and could not control, and these were priorities for me as the manager to focus on in order to make life easier for the team. We then made pasta which no one had done before. Made it together, ate it together and took a cab home together which was a nice experience. It was not competitive activity and no one was better than anyone else because we had to rely on each other for the different stages. It helped to remove the divide between front-of-house and backroom workers.

Manager, private sector

Avoid the mistake of simply adding up available days minus holidays. Ensure that you create the space for learning, thinking and team-building too. Use this as the basis of saying 'no'. One of the most underused words in any manager's vocabulary. Not 'no' for the sake of it. 'No' because there isn't the capacity to do that. Or alternatively, what is it that you would like us to stop doing in order to accommodate that?

Six tips for leading your team

1. Invest time with new joiners to build trust.

2. Anything that prevents your team from excelling should be your top priority.

3. If you're planning a team-building event, choose an activity that no one has done before so that you're all learning together.

4. Get your newest team member to revise or rewrite the induction after they've been through it to keep it relevant.

5. Send a handwritten note or card before a new team member joins.

6. Rewards such as increased autonomy, flexible working hours, recognition and development opportunities are powerful motivators.

Questions to reflect on

1. Have you ever had a 'get to know you' conversation with your boss which is mutual? If not, why not?

2. Do you trust first or do people need to earn your trust? What does that mean for how you engage with others?

3. If someone from another area was to ask a member of your team what their purpose was, what do you think their answer would be? Is that what you want it to be?

4. Have you co-created an overt team culture with all of your team members? If so, how do you measure performance against this?

5. Do you have a team which has sufficient diversity of experience and thought? Does your team feel like a place of groupthink or constructive challenge?

6. What can you do to normalize the process of feedback in your interactions – with your direct reports, your team and your manager?

Resources

Creating psychological safety

Professor Amy Edmonson is an expert in this area having written *The fearless organization* (Wiley, 2018). In this article, she talks about how psychological safety takes off the brakes that keep people from achieving what's possible and includes The Leader's Tool Kit for Building Psychological Safety. www.strategy-business.com/article/How-Fearless-Organizations-Succeed?gko=63131

Trust and vulnerability

Brené Brown is an expert on authenticity and vulnerability. In addition to her book *Dare to lead* (Vermillion, 2018), her website has a worksheet titled *Rising strong truth and dare: an introduction* which can be found in the *Dare to lead* downloads, https://brenebrown.com/downloads/

Co-creating culture

This is a simple exercise for co-creating culture within an existing team, and has the added benefit of proving that culture is not a soft subject! The main components can be done in around 30 minutes. It's quick and highly effective.

Step 1 – setting up the exercise

- Split your team into at least pairs or up to groups of four, depending on the size.
- Give them each a large piece of flipchart paper and pens.
- Ask them to draw a line down the centre of the paper and create two columns, one headed 'Positive' and the other 'Negative'.
- Feel free to wander around the groups, engaging and encouraging them between each step.

Step 2 – Part 1 of the task

- Ask the teams to spend 3 minutes brainstorming the positive and negative features of the current culture using only descriptive adjectives – single words are preferable.
- Encourage them to be open and candid, it is a safe space for sharing.
- Remind them not to censor their thinking or spend too long debating the words – this is a quick-fire brainstorm.

Step 3 – Part 2 of the task

Once the 3 minutes is up, explain to the groups that you're not going to dwell on the words in the positive column, but that this next part of the task will focus on those they've listed in the negative column.

- Ask the teams to spend a further 5 minutes looking at each of the negative words on the list and to consider what that means for the performance of their team or the organization.
- They annotate their list with each of these impacts.
- Ask them to be specific about the impact, e.g. they can't just say 'it's a bit rubbish', it should be more like 'we're slow to make decisions', or 'we're slow to market', or 'it extends the length of time it takes to recruit people'. The important thing is that the impact has to be tangible.

Step 4 – Part 3 of the task

The last part of the exercise is the most challenging – you give them a further 5 minutes for this and ask them to now put an estimate on the cost of that impact to the organization. Explain that this doesn't have to be exact and that broad estimates are fine.

Step 5 – Task plenary and conclusions

At the end of the three parts of the exercise, ask the groups to reflect on the list of negative features. Begin to highlight the fact that some of them are about behaviours, but others are about things like processes, rules, policies – use some examples from what you have seen on the flipcharts. And to illustrate the first part of the conclusions:

Culture = behaviours + infrastructure

Remind the groups that when thinking about culture, people automatically default to behaviours, but what they've all demonstrated is that the organizational infrastructure also has a part to play in supporting and shaping culture. For example, there is no point sending teams on training to learn the right behaviours to empower their teams and then returning to an organization where the policies and processes prevent them from putting that into action.

Ask for an indication of some of the costs of the negative aspects of the culture the groups have identified. Encourage people to think about this as they are shared. Use this to illustrate the second part of the conclusion:

Culture is *not* a soft subject

Make the point to the groups that not only does it have a quantifiable drag factor on your performance, the counterargument is true – it has a quantifiable accelerating impact on your performance when you get it right. So a clear return on investment case can be created for investing time and resources into changing your culture. It is as crucial to business performance as cash and assets, and is not something that HR do!

Step 6 – Shaping team culture

Having proved the points about why it matters and the type of features you need to think about, you can now facilitate a discussion about what you want the culture to feel like in that team – as one group or in smaller groups with a plenary. The important thing is that it is co-created.

You then promise, as the leader of that team, to take that away and synthesize it into a set of clear commitment statements for the team and return with a final draft for comment.

Keeping this alive through what you do as a manager, how you provide feedback and hold each other to account against it, and challenging ways of working which don't align with your team commitment statement is your next job.

You can adapt this exercise if you don't have an existing team to work with. For a brand new team people can think about positive and negative features from organizations and teams they have worked for in the past which still enables you to prove the point about why it matters and then shape your desired culture together.

© Innermost Consulting. Reproduced with permission.
www.innermost-consulting.com/

High-performing teams

This TED Talk from Margaret Heffernan is a salient reminder of why IQ in teams is not important but helpfulness and personal interconnectedness are. She is compelling on the importance of taking time to build social capital in teams, www.youtube.com/watch?v=1-PazvfN9EU

Notes

[1] *Edelman Trust Barometer 2020*, www.edelman.co.uk/research/edelman-trust-barometer-2020 [accessed 15 December 2020].

[2] Lucy Adams, *HR disrupted* (Practical Inspiration, 2017).

[3] *The five keys to a successful Google team*, https://rework.withgoogle.com/blog/five-keys-to-a-successful-google-team [accessed 15 December 2020].

[4] Daniel Coyle, *The culture code* (Penguin Random House, 2018).

[5] Brené Brown, *Dare to lead* (Vermillion, 2018). See also https://brenebrown.com for free resources [accessed 15 December 2020].

[6] Jack Zenger and Joseph Folkman, 'The ideal praise-to-criticism ratio', *Harvard Business Review online* (2013), https://hbr.org/2013/03/the-ideal-praise-to-criticism [accessed 15 December 2020].

[7] The surprising truth about what motivates us is revealed in an animated presentation by Daniel Pink at the RSA www.youtube.com/watch?v=u6XAPnuFjJc [accessed 15 December 2020].

[8] Matthew Syed, *Rebel power* (John Murray, 2019).

7 Having difficult conversations

Why it matters

We all dread difficult conversations. That's often because issues have been left to fester. But every manager will have to do this at some point in their career. The difference between doing it well and doing it badly has a profound impact on individuals and wider performance. Getting it right makes handling exits easier, if that's where things end up.

This chapter will take you through the building blocks for doing this well, spanning feedback, expectations and how to let people go.

Managing performance is one of the things we're asked for help with most frequently. And failing to deal with poor performance is one of the greatest irritations cited by team members. But people dread it – generally because they are doing it from a position of performance not being where it needs to be. And this is further undermined by the rarity of feedback being the norm. In some cases, the fear of having the conversation can be greater than the reality.

But if you treat the management of performance as a positive, intrinsic part of your management practice, making it a good habit, then when it's not where it should be it's less of a hurdle for you to encounter. So let's start with the basics.

The desire to preserve harmony prevents difficult conversations with people and holding them accountable.

Manager, public sector

Feedback as the foundation

Feedback. Why is it that word creates a sense of fear whenever most people hear it? That slightly sarcastic inference that feedback is a gift, when the process of providing and receiving it is one of the things that most people dread.

Like all things that we do, those that become habitual get easier. And like all habits, that starts with practice. When you think about all areas of your management and leadership practice you'll find some things which just come so naturally that when you're asked how you do it, you really have to stop and think about it, as it is so well ingrained that it has become a subconscious competence. In others, you'll have had to practice and learn from experience – especially when things haven't gone well – and it's much more of a conscious competence that you step through every time you do it.

In our experience, a true culture of feedback is rarely seen in organizations, largely due to the dread that the word creates, so the habit doesn't get formed and the viral impact of learning from each other continuously is lost. Which is such a shame. Feedback isn't just a gift, it is – as Boris Becker once said – the breakfast of champions. How can we know what we're doing well and where we need to improve if no one tells us? Where are the opportunities for personal development and growth if that insight is denied?

Think about your own experience. How many times have you worked in a team when it's obvious that someone is being carried by others, yet no one is addressing this? Can you remember the impact? The drain on morale and motivation of the rest of the team. The resentment that builds. The feelings of negativity that this creates towards that individual.

It works the same way for star performers. Those people doing well, but rarely having their contribution acknowledged. Having no opportunities to celebrate their success. No visibility for their achievements in a way that might aid their development or career progression. There is a palpable dip in motivation caused by this, both for the individual and their contribution to the team.

Not only does this have a detrimental impact on the individuals concerned, it also undermines the team cohesion. It creates an implicit acceptance of a reduced sense of transparency and openness. An unwillingness to tackle difficult issues. Which ultimately starts to reduce the value that group of people adds, no longer being greater than the sum of their parts in whatever endeavour they're applying themselves to.

If you accept the premise that culture is an accelerant of performance, it's our belief that cultures with excellent feedback practice at their heart are those that make the biggest difference. Conversations between managers and direct reports are richer and more valuable. Successes are acknowledged and captured. Areas for improvement can be coached and supported. Where we've seen it work well in all types of teams, there has been an overt conversation between team members as to both the importance of feedback and how they'll hold each other to account. There are some suggestions for principles and mechanisms to support feedback at the end of the chapter.

Here's an example from a team, newly formed on the back of an organization in crisis. They had overt conversations about how they wanted to work together. What behaviours and contributions they wanted from each other. And how they'd hold each other to account for that. They recognized they were a new group and it would take time to reach the level of team maturity to create the conditions they needed to do this well. So they started with post-meeting online evaluations. They embedded two-way feedback between the manager of the team and each individual as the norm in their meetings. That saw them progress to a dedicated feedback session after each meeting, where they provided in-the-moment observations to each other on how they'd done against the standards they agreed for themselves. Until they reached a point when someone said in the meeting 'I don't want to wait for the feedback session at the end to say this...' Magic!

It took conscious effort and commitment from everyone involved, but it created a new set of habits which deepened and strengthened their ways of working, until it became so innate it didn't need a dedicated session for feedback to become the norm. The benefits of this? It significantly accelerated the impact of that team as they were continuously improving all the time. It meant they were adding incrementally more value to the organization every time they came together. And it had the radiated benefit of deepening their rapport and working relationships, valuing new insights and building respect. It made dissonance of views acceptable, encouraging those people with different perspectives to speak up. That dissonance created productive tension, that led to better problem-solving and strategizing. The list goes on. All because they committed to making feedback part of their practice and did so with positive intent.

Case study: The power of feedback – better late than never

I was working with a private equity-backed start-up with grand ambitions. Many of the senior team were current or previous heavy-hitters from the corporate world. A Finance Director was appointed to keep an eye on the significant tens of millions pounds that had been invested.

The founder was innately creative and brilliant at what he did. To give you an idea of how non-corporate he was, he dismissed the title of CEO in favour of 'Gardener of the Dream Orchard'. Many of the initial team getting the business off the ground were similarly creative and not corporate.

Whenever there were workshops or events to shape or design the offer, every time the Finance Director contributed it was described as being like a Dementor from the Harry Potter books – sucking all the life and energy from the room. I noticed the team complaining about him. Then saw similar complaints about his approach and the impact in other forums. Yet no one was giving him feedback. When I challenged them on this, it was clear that very experienced people didn't want to have the conversation. They weren't comfortable doing it so let the issue fester.

On one such occasion the impact of his behaviour was so profound that he finally noticed it too. He was curious and, as he left the room, clearly felt the need to validate this thought with someone, so turned to the person next to him. That someone happened to be the first week in first job PA to the CEO (or Gardener of the Dream Orchard).

He asked her if she had noticed what had happened in the room. And without hesitating, but with due kindness and compassion, she gave him the feedback that his much more experienced peers and colleagues had failed to give him for the preceding six months.

This led to a discussion between us about how that was the first time anyone had ever given him feedback on his behaviour in his over 30 years at work. He committed to doing something about it, worked with a coach, and the negative impact of his contributions became positive. The power of feedback... and the consequences of the cowardice of not providing it in one simple experience.

The importance of clear expectations

One of the most common reasons why performance conversations are so difficult is because there hasn't been an overt discussion about expectations, support requirements and how success will be measured. Where annual objective setting is undertaken, it's rarely done in a meaningful way or revisited at any point between then and the next appraisal. We're not suggesting for one moment that having a conversation which agrees the top priorities for the year ahead isn't important – especially the developmental component – but setting expectations should be done on a much more regular basis as part of all tasking. If that sounds onerous, it doesn't need to be.

You're having a conversation with a member of your team and you ask them to pick up a particular task or project. More often than not, that's the sum total of the conversation: 'I'd really like you to take the lead on x,' or, 'I'd like you to work with y to deliver z.' Now let's try that conversation slightly differently...

'I'd really like you to take the lead on x, let's grab 30 minutes to talk it through.' In those 30 minutes you provide a proper set of requirements for the solution you're asking to be delivered. What problem are you trying to solve, what would a good outcome look like, where can you see potential pitfalls and opportunities? While also recognizing that more will emerge in the undertaking of the task – so these will need revisiting. Who else might need to be involved or engaged with, what timeframe does it need to be done in? Classic framing using *why, what, how, who* and *when*. This is always done best conversationally, co-creating and owning the outcome jointly. At the end of that conversation, you can recap the headlines: why the task needs doing, what it'll involve, some initial thoughts on considerations for how you might manage it, who should be engaged with and when it needs to be done by.

Now think about every time someone hasn't delivered for you and you need to manage their performance. How much easier would it be to do that if this kind of conversation had taken place at the outset? No opportunities for 'it wasn't clear', 'it wasn't explained to me', or 'I didn't understand'. You have shared and transparent clarity from the outset. And the time it takes to do that is a tiny fraction of the time that would be consumed managing something which lacked that clarity further down the line.

Those inputs are the foundation for any tasking activity with a team member, but it's only part of the expectation setting. You might be giving someone a stretch into a new area to support their development. You might be embarking on something new for the organization or the team. They might need some support to help them. And you should always ask that question as a courtesy anyway – it signals your willingness to provide it, to develop capability, and sets the tone for a culture where it's OK to ask for help.

You should also agree how you're going to measure success – along the way or at the end. The SMART acronym – Specific, Measurable, Achievable, Realistic and Time-bound – might be helpful here. Whatever tool you use, the important thing is that expectations are clear, explicitly stated and you should be able to objectively assess progress. If it's something that will take several weeks or months then how often do you think it would be useful to check in on progress? And when? At key points on the journey or a regulated frequency? These provide opportunities for feedback and further support, plus the ability to respond to any changes in context or new learning which might require you to reframe the expectations. This can be an iterative or one-off process.

Having agreed the feedback points in advance, you now need to use them wisely! Never wing it, always be prepared. Think about the questions you want to ask. Keep a note of unsolicited feedback you might hear from other team members or stakeholders.

Those feedback sessions are vital. For the individual to provide an update on where they're at. This is their chance to shine. Their moment to ask for help. Maybe their moment to bury bad news or hide the true status of things. You need to be prepared for all of these – with praise, compassion and curiosity.

They require active listening on your part. Don't be afraid to play back what you hear to avoid misinterpretation or misunderstanding. Say it out loud and ask 'have I got that right?'. Allow them the chance to refine or comment until you both have absolute clarity on meaning and emphasis. Are you hearing evidence or excuses? Have you compared your views with any other reference points you might have? Have you considered the quality not only of what's being done, but how it's being done? There may be great task performance with poor behavioural performance or vice versa. Remember to be constructive and to always provide feedback with positive intent. The kind of honesty that comes from positive intent, rather than negative criticism, is what generates greater performance. Responsible people will thrive on, and are worthy of, that freedom. But mainly this is about asking open questions.

Case study: The power of open questions

I'd been managing people and poor performance for over 20 years and thought I was pretty good at it. Then I had a development intervention that made me realize the power of asking open questions. As managers, we tend to have made up our mind about where performance is at before we go into the room. We also have a tendency to want to fix the problem or just get the task which is falling behind done. All human nature. But this is a real barrier to managing performance well.

Asking open, leading questions which support the individual in deepening their understanding of why there's an issue, what they need to do about it, and the consequences of not doing so, is so much more powerful.

Take everything you were going to say and reframe it into a question. Turn 'I've had feedback from x person that you aren't going about things in the right way', into 'Why do you think x person is finding it challenging working with you on this project?'. Keep asking why, as they give you their evidence or excuses. It completely changes the dynamic. It places the ownership for their performance on themselves. And it's just as powerful for making good performers great.

The key about these conversations is they enable you to create a virtuous cycle. It is an opportunity to provide ongoing feedback rather than waiting until the end of the task. It is an opportunity to iterate and refine the expectations or the support that's required. It is an opportunity to intervene to minimize the impact of underperformance, but in a way where the responsibility for that is clearly owned by the individual. And most importantly, if you conclude that the individual is never going to make the grade, you have more than one opportunity to effect that change.

That's why you should always create space to think and prepare for these conversations, and always follow them up with simple action points or reframing of what's been agreed. Not full notes, rather a summary that constantly provides the same clarity that you started with when you first set the expectations.

This is valuable for you and the individual. You need to create the space to think about what you're learning from having given this individual the task to complete. Have you given it to the right person? Are you realizing that they're the right person but in the wrong role? What are they learning about themselves – are you asking them that in your feedback check-ins?

Following these steps ensures that you can frame, steer and reflect throughout someone's performance journey. Doing a year-end appraisal process should be a walk in the park, as you've been doing it iteratively throughout the year. You're just formalizing what has become custom and practice about the way you manage your people. They're as relevant for a star performer as a poor performer. It provides objectivity for that trickiest of performance management challenges – the mediocre performer. It's the DNA for good performance management. And it avoids getting to that point where something's gone wrong and you try to do all this retrospectively, which almost always leads to dispute and recriminations.

It takes time, but not lots of time, and (at the risk of repeating ourselves) saves you much more in the long run. And it's your job, remember. Your job is to create an environment that allows people to be the best version of themselves. Helping to manage their development and performance is an integral part of this.

If you take only one thing away from this chapter, let it be this: never compromise on a proper conversation when setting up a new task or moving people into a new role. Clear expectations, agreed support, measures of success and feedback points. If you have those foundations, managing performance just got so much easier.

Dignified exits: letting people go with clarity and kindness

So what happens when you've done everything you should, but performance just isn't where it needs to be – task or behaviour or both? How often have you got to this point and known that it's not working out but you convince yourself that it'll somehow miraculously get better? Or that you don't have enough evidence or audit trail to let them go?

If you accept the principle that the biggest determinant of performance is your people, then you can't afford to carry passengers in your team. It's not fair on them, the organization or the wider team. Our research tells us that one of the greatest irritants to managers is the failure to manage poor performance. Everyone can see when someone is underperforming relative to them and others. The drain on morale and motivation that this causes is corrosive, which creates a further drag factor on performance. Not dealing with this creates a vicious negative cycle.

Very often, managers prevent themselves from doing anything about it because they feel guilty. Or are simply fearful of having to do this kind of thing. But in most situations its no one's fault. Interviews are a notoriously unreliable predictor of on the job performance, so of course it won't work out all the time. It can be about style and fit as much as about their competence – task or behaviour. Your responsibility as a manager is to have done the right things. Providing feedback and being clear about what improvements you expect. Putting in place support prior to discussing a formal personal improvement plan will give them time to reflect and consider whether they want to make the choice to leave. And to be able to have a conversation where there is clarity that, as performance hasn't improved, it is time to accept that things still aren't working. Ignoring or pretending that this isn't the case isn't helpful.

Your role is to ensure there's both clarity and kindness in the exit. We're assuming you did all the right things in terms of providing feedback and managing performance to give you, and them, the objective evidence base that things aren't as they should be. If this is the case then the conversation really shouldn't come as a big surprise

That doesn't mean that clarity isn't required. We've seen lots of people fudge language in the way that people do in any difficult situation. Think about when someone dies. They *passed on, passed away, went to a better place*. They rarely *died* or are *dead*. It is human nature to soften and couch language when delivering difficult messages. But that isn't helpful. If anything it makes the process harder.

Prepare for the conversation well. Use your words sparingly. Create space so that every word has chance to land. Don't soften your language so there can be any room for misunderstanding. Kim Scott's *Radical candour* has some great insights on this and is signposted at the end of the chapter. Be in no doubt in your messaging: this hasn't worked out, so it's time for them to leave the organization. Recognize your own responsibility in the situation and acknowledge that all things start with the best of intentions but that it hasn't worked out. Be ready to have the key reasons why that's the case. Always separate people and personalities from the problems that have led to this point. And never get into a situation where blame features. Blame is subjective and blurs the objectivity that clarity requires. This is a factual situation. It's not working for these reasons.

Clarity is only half of the equation. Clarity is required for the message, to ensure it is heard and understood. Kindness is the other half. This is a human being whose livelihood you are temporarily ending. However many conversations have been precursors to this one, however aware they are that this is coming, the actual news will still be a shock. Kindness doesn't mean watering down the message, quite the opposite. Providing objective, open and clear messaging is a kindness in itself. The kindness is about having empathy and putting yourself in their shoes. How will they be feeling? Do they need some time to process the information? Might they need a break in the conversation and to return to it? How can you frame the clarity empathetically? For example, you could say: 'I need to have a conversation with you today that I appreciate you may find challenging, so just say if you want to stop or take a break at any point.'

It is possible to have these kinds of conversations in a way which is respectful and enables you to maintain a good relationship after this point. Show that you have a genuine desire for them to move on success-fully. This is advantageous for a number of reasons. You never know when your paths may cross again. And just because it hasn't worked out in this role, in this organization, doesn't mean that they don't have value to add in the right role at the right time. You may be able to find options for mutual gain – you may know someone in your network or sector who's looking for someone like this person. But most impor-tantly of all, it is recognition that acting and behaving with humanity, no matter the situation, is something we all appreciate.

Questions to reflect on

1. Do you always set clear expectations when tasking your team? If not, what gets in the way?

2. Do you set aside time to think about the performance of your team members on a regular basis and not just at the annual appraisal window?

3. Do you have a tendency to tell people what is going wrong and/or offer solutions? What would help you approach this with a more open, questioning style that helps people get to the conclusion themselves and own their performance?

4. How often have you avoided moving someone on who you know isn't performing? What's been the impact on you, your team and performance?

5. When you've had these conversations and they haven't gone well, what did you learn from that?

6. What can you do to exercise your responsibility to provide clarity and kindness to someone in a situation like this?

Resources

Managing performance – a holistic approach

When you are managing performance, it's essential to keep the balance between task and behavioural performance when you are providing feedback – the *how* and the *what* working well together. How many times have you seen the negative impact not of what someone has done technically, but how they've gone about it? We want these two working well to create a multiplier effect on performance, as this task and behaviour grid made famous by Jack Welch of General Electric shows.

High		
	This person has a neutral or negative effect on organizational performance	**This person has a 'multiplier' effect on organizational performance**
	This person has a negative effect on organizational performance	**This person has a neutral or negative effect on organizational performance**

Functional/task performance (vertical axis, from Low to High)

Low

High

Inappropriate /negative impact on others' performance — **Behavioural performance** — Appropriate /positive impact on others' performance

It's fairly obvious that someone operating in the bottom left quadrant is going to be having a negative impact on performance – technically weak at their job and difficult to work with too. What often surprises people is the negative impact of people in the bottom right and top left quadrants. The person on the bottom right will be a delight to be around, but that joy will soon wear off when they fail to deliver anything or if they do, it isn't to the appropriate quality.

The top left is what we call brilliant but challenging. Those incredible experts in their field who are very difficult to work with, which soon undermines the impact of their specialist field of expertise.

When managing performance you want to be driving good or great performance in both dimensions so your team are in the top right quadrant. This creates a multiplier effect. Not just from their own performance but because people operating at that level tend to enable their teams to do the same, and this has a positive ripple effect.

When managing those in the top left quadrant, you need to be resolute about the fact that you work in an environment or culture where their impact on team performance cannot be tolerated, and that they may be better suited to a different organization.

When managing those in the bottom right quadrant, you need to be clear about the fact that you work in an environment or culture in which hard work without results cannot be tolerated, and wish them luck in the rest of their career.

And for those in the bottom left corner, if following the principles of good performance management in this section doesn't have the requisite boost in their performance, you have to be clear that this isn't working out.

When this gets hard, there are some good tests you can use as you apply this framework:

- For your team: which of my people, if they told me they were leaving, would I fight hard to keep?
- For yourself: if you told your boss you were leaving, how hard would they fight to keep you? And if you don't know the answer to that question, what stops you asking them?

Feedback principles and mechanisms

It is always best to agree the principles underpinning why you would want to give feedback across the team before introducing the practice.

This creates a deeper understanding of the value and importance of feedback. It also provides the opportunity to generate commitment and ownership to this being a core part of your team culture.

Principles

These could include demonstrable commitments such as:

- Have the courage to ask for and be willing to give each other feedback, regardless of role.
- Feedback will be provided constructively, with positive intent: be specific and do so often and in a timely way.
- Say thank you when we hear feedback, without defending, allowing ourselves to digest before responding.
- Be brave enough to act on feedback provided.

Mechanisms

These will vary depending on context, but they tend to span the following four types:

- In the moment, on a one-to-one basis.
- Reviewed at the end of each formal meeting against the stated team culture.
- Core part of the agenda whenever the whole team comes together.
- Actively requested from other teams and/or senior people who they interact with regularly.

Giving challenging feedback

Kim Scott coined the term *Radical candour* (Macmillan, 2017) as the title for her book describing guidance and feedback that's both kind and clear, specific and sincere. The Radical Candour website also has a range of informative podcasts and blogs, which you can find at www.radicalcandor.com/our-approach

8 Meeting madness

Why it matters

Meetings are the bane of most people's working lives. A bold statement, but not a surprise when you consider our research showed that people spend between a staggering third to three-quarters of their working time in meetings. If we all got better at this, the impact on us and those we work with would be exponential. Productive and engaging meetings feels like a good goal for us all!

And it wasn't just the quantity of meetings that was such a striking finding from our research, but the quality of them too. Frustration with meetings was one of the strongest issues that emerged, across all sectors and role types. Frequency, length, duplication. Every aspect. Some sectors were more beset by the curse of pointless meetings than others, but it is a common feature, and got us thinking about how great the world of work would be if every meeting was purposeful, productive and you left the room feeling like it was a fantastic use of your time! So why does it so often feel like the opposite? Are people skilled in the art of a good meeting? Is there sufficient accountability for the quality of the meeting? Or an established feedback mechanism to drive improvement? Is everyone really present or are they checking emails or daydreaming about the things they would rather be doing?

You might not be in control of all the meetings you attend, but you can at least take charge of the ones that you run. There's a resource at the end of this chapter which might help you with this, but in the meantime here's our blueprint.

I can find myself having spent all day in meetings then finding it's 5 o'clock before I can start my day.

Manager, private sector

Purpose

It sounds obvious to be clear about the purpose of the meeting, but how many have you sat through where you have wondered what the point is? Exactly. Our favourite sport in those situations is to mentally calculate the cost of that pointlessness – there's always too many people and it goes on for too long. If you were paying for that meeting out of your own pocket, you wouldn't tolerate it for a moment more than you had to!

There should only be four reasons for any meeting taking place:

- Shaping: creative sessions to generate ideas or innovate.
- Teambuilding: activities which will build trust and rapport across a group of people.
- Governance or decision-making: Boards, committees, steering groups.
- Management: one-to-one meetings with direct reports to support performance and development.

If it's not any of these things, then why get people together? And please don't say to update people on what's happening – there are countless more effective mechanisms for tracking progress, including short daily stand-ups, or you can incorporate updates into any of the four categories above, so long as you don't let that become the dominant purpose.

The agenda should reflect the purpose of the meeting. Don't fall into the trap of just opening the last agenda and then updating it – we've seen that happen a lot in the NHS with Board meeting agendas where, even allowing for the statutory agenda items, habit drives the need for a three-hour meeting.

Before you schedule a meeting, be clear about its purpose. If it's not obvious, think about whether you need it. If it is, communicate it with attendees, and make sure you stick to it once you are in the room.

Preparation

There is a mountain of research that says the optimum number of people for a good meeting is six to eight, and definitely never more than ten. If you choose your attendees wisely based on what input you need and not on what job title or position they hold, six to eight should be plenty to create sufficient diversity of input, a wide range of views and good decisions.

Never invite people just because you ought to or you want them to see what happens. What a waste of everyone's time! It's the in-person version of the curse of an email cc which was a major issue for all of our research participants. We know email overload harms productivity due to the distraction factor. Some forward-thinking companies will try and address this through footnotes on their messages, e.g., 'At XXX we work flexibly – so while it suits me to email now, I do not expect any response or action outside of your own working pattern.' That's great, but it still doesn't stop the volume of emails. So here's some handy rules to minimise them.

If you're sending an email to just one person, stop typing and have a conversation. Get up and go and talk to them or pick up the phone.

I don't really understand why you have to be on that conference call, when you know you haven't got anything to add and you're not going to say anything. It doesn't make sense why you have to take your time to be part of it, which is really frustrating.

Manager, public sector

You know those long-winded emails that make you think what is this about? You read it through twice and still aren't sure what it's asking you. So I pick up the phone and just ask them to explain it to me. We should just use the phone more.

Manager, third sector

If you have information that you need to send to more than one person, send the email, but only to those who need to see it. And never use cc – why are you doing that? To show that you've done the work? To cover your back? To save yourself having to tell that person? All bad reasons. You don't need to show inputs, when outputs and outcomes are what matters. You're perpetuating a negative culture if you are back-covering. And you're missing out on an opportunity to build rapport and develop a positive working relationship with someone when you avoid a conversation. Rant over.

So, when you think about meeting attendees, delete everyone who's metaphorically a cc on your list. There's no point in inviting anyone who might sit there and say nothing. If they're not a key contributor to the purpose, they shouldn't be there.

Once you've got your perfect list of attendees, think of it as the guest list to an event for which you are the host. Make sure you are attentive to creating a good experience. Seating, refreshments, room temperature. Get into the mindset of accepting that you are taking people away from their other work so you want the experience to be as productive as it can be.

Only people actually involved in the project are invited and meetings are bite-sized, 15 minutes. Team meetings are lessons learned, what went well and what didn't go so well so that everyone can learn, not the day-to-day workload.

Manager, third sector

Again, there's a mountain of research that says that people's energy and intellectual capacity decreases after 30 minutes, wanes after an hour, and is done at two. Now you might know people who are exceptions to that rule, but if you can't achieve the purpose of your meeting in two hours, then you've probably got too much on the agenda. In some cases, 15 minutes might be enough. Meetings will expand to fit the time. Don't give them the space to do this.

Think about the purpose. Be clinical about what's required when constructing the agenda, as this drives the duration, as well as the outcomes you need to deliver for the purpose of the meeting.

Style

It would be easy to think the purpose of the meeting dictates the style, but that's overly simplistic. Your decision-making meeting might be a 15-minute daily stand-up which prioritizes your work for the day. It could be a formal Board meeting with papers and big investment decisions to make. The style of the meeting is determined by three things:

1. The person leading or chairing the meeting: they set the tone, drive the outputs, keep people focused on the purpose and encourage contributions from everyone. They need to get people in the right frame of mind by greeting people positively, allowing them to exit where their mind was and settle into the purpose of what you are doing together. Any gathering of people has a social function to it too, so allow people to connect and bond in the informal chat before the meeting starts.

2. Behaviours of attendees: this is facilitated by the way the Chair manages the meeting (and any framing provided in advance), how people engage with the subject matter and are motivated around the purpose, and most vitally of all – how prepared people are

for the meeting itself. There are practical things you can do like agreeing to close lids on laptops or having a no phones rule – President Obama was famed for not allowing phones into his meetings. If that is a step too far, carve out short breaks for people to check their phones while ensuring that alerts are turned off during the meeting.

3. Feedback: things only improve when you have feedback – asking for it at the end of meetings helps you get better at them. It shows you are curious and role models a growth mindset. Always much better to have that feedback to work on than everyone talking about it among themselves and you being none the wiser! And as your meetings become more productive and enjoyable, provide that feedback to others and influence them to do the same with their colleagues.

The brilliant Graham Allcott of Think Productive reminded us of the HiPPO effect in meetings. This is the phenomenon of everyone deferring to the highest paid person in the room.[1] While these participants add value, their presence is also a risk as their status means that their influence might prevent the most useful ideas from ever being heard. As a manager, sometimes you will be the HiPPO, and he suggests the following ways in which you can lessen the potential for you having a negative impact:

- Consciously make the decision to speak last in the group, so the tone is firmly set without you.
- Be humble and brief in your contributions.
- Ask more questions than you give answers.
- Dish out lots of praise for other people's ideas.
- Create a space for healthy dissent, analysis and disagreement.
- Remember the old Harry Truman quote, 'It's amazing what you can accomplish if you do not care who gets the credit'.

Tips to try

1. Before the meeting starts formally, get everyone to turn off notifications or ensure their devices are set to silent – sounds obvious but it still happens and distracts the entire meeting.

2. Periodically scrap the agenda and ask everyone to talk about the outcome you're aiming for and what you want to achieve.

3. If you're discussing a difficult issue that's causing stress, take a break to let people talk informally to others and relieve the tension.

4. Try a daily stand-up – a 10–15 minute mini meeting for those directly involved in delivery of a task or project: a quick round the room on your wins from the previous day, your priorities for the day ahead and the opportunity to flag something you need help from others on.

5. Think about how the requirements might differ if you are meeting online:

    •   Work with your team to produce an etiquette for online meetings.

    •   Ask all participants to check the tech is working five minutes before the start time.

    •   Maintaining concentration can be difficult, so plan to keep meetings as short as possible.

    •   Ensure all other devices are switched off.

    •   When planning the agenda, ensure there are only one or two complex issues and allow frequent short breaks from the screen to counter tiredness, ideally two or three minutes every half hour.

    •   Avoid multi-tasking on a video call – it sets a bad example and can cause cognitive overload.

    •   If people cannot attend, ask them to do a brief video update related to the agenda.

    •   Hiding the image of yourself can reduce feelings of self-consciousness.

Questions to reflect on

1. How often do you find yourself in a meeting thinking, there's another x hours of my life I'm never getting back? What is it that causes you to feel like that?

2. When was the last time you looked at your standing meeting schedule in your diary and questioned the purpose, relevance and value of them? What can you do about that?

3. How can you set a new shared standard for meetings as part of your team culture?

Resources

Why meetings go wrong and how to fix them

Managers are rarely trained in the art of effective meetings. Professor Steven Rosenberg explains how leaders can improve them in this podcast interview based on his book *The surprising science of meetings: how you can lead your team to peak performance,* https://hbr.org/podcast/2019/11/why-meetings-go-wrong-and-how-to-fix-them

Notes

[1] *Think Productive,* https://thinkproductive.co.uk/about/productivity-keynote-talks-delivered-exclusively-by-graham-allcott [accessed 15 December 2020].

9 Epilogue: So what next... a new normal?

We felt compelled to write this book because it seemed that these eight challenges were universal. Timeless classics if you will. Regardless of organization type, sectors or the relative experience of managers. Our research told us that if there was support to accelerate learning for managers in these areas, they would have the biggest impact on their performance, motivation and morale.

But as we say right at the start of this book, context is king, and there is no doubt that while the people elements in the second part of the book are universal, the operating context we talk about at the start has changed in recent years. The level of ambiguity. Greater collaboration – within and across organizations. The acceleration of the rate of change, which is only getting faster. We now have smartphones in our pockets which are often more powerful than the laptops we carry around. As that computing power, artificial intelligence and other technology-driven innovation has developed further, we now have an app for everything, directions to anywhere, the means to buy anything we want at any time of the day, and to be connected to our work 24/7. As these developments continue to advance at an exponential rate, our environment within organizations and society will continue to have to adapt. And, as ever, some will get there faster than others.

The coronavirus pandemic has put a rocket booster under already emerging trends, none more so than online working. Vigorously championed by many sections of society for years, necessity suddenly brought about that change on a universal basis. There are clear benefits for employees in respect of increased flexibility and quality of life. And for employers in terms of lower costs of doing business with smaller overheads for office accommodation. While online working will be a part of our lives forever, the degree to which it remains when we emerge from the pandemic is still questionable. A survey by Barclays has shown that while employers and employees like working from home – and intend to do so more in the future – only 10% expect to do so permanently.

The survey suggests that working two to three days a week from home will become the norm for up to half of the working population.[1]

I'm never going back to an office for more than three days a week.

Manager, private sector

Nevertheless, important decisions about the future of organizations will now increasingly be made in a virtual environment – first through necessity and now convenience. What does that mean for the quality of those choices given the limitations of technology and the ability to engage with each other that this creates?

We've focused on navigating ambiguity and uncertainty as perennial challenges, and these features have been exacerbated by recent events. Doubt and uncertainty have become constants, and the ability to plan with confidence has been even further undermined. Annual plans and budgets have been thrown into disarray. Managers have had to navigate uncertainty for their teams while facing an uncertain future of their own. The greater the uncertainty, the more we seek people with answers – the old type of heroic leaders. The truth is, there is no one with all the answers in such unprecedented circumstances. So our encouragement to focus on preparedness takes on an even greater sense of importance. Underpinned by sound assumptions informing decisions, regularly revisiting them as circumstances change.

So how will we lead our people in this brave new world? People-centred leadership has been evolving for decades, but has had to come to the fore to accommodate not only this changing context, but the shift in societal expectations about the purpose of work for us as individuals. We can see how these changes have iterated over the course of several generations. But as with all trends, sometimes we get a sudden paradigm shift brought about by an external influence. And the coronavirus pandemic has certainly provided one of those.

Does it change any of the fundamental challenges we set out in this book? No. But it does cause us to reflect on how we might need to deploy the tools and techniques we've provided. How do you operate as a people-centred leader when you are not in close proximity with your people? The fundamentals of everything we describe as essential to getting the best out of others are unchanged. But what is it that you need to be aware of as we enter what is surely the new normal?

No one is missing the less attractive features of their commute – crowded, late-running public transport or traffic-jammed roads aren't being mourned. But they are missing the transition and boundary it created at the start or end of the day. Maybe the reading or podcast listening that they used the time for. Work–life balance might be improved for some. Quality time with family enhanced. It is now eminently possible for many in management roles to work from home, and may even be preferable for some people. So leading and managing remote teams is here to stay.

How do we manage the fact that all of us – even the most strident introverts – are social creatures who miss interacting with other humans? The ability to create and build connections with others over a shared purpose or interest. And it is this that isn't happening. Those small, almost invisible acts that create trust among individuals and teams.

Simon Sinek has observed that while working virtually might be more convenient, there's no substitute for human contact.[2] And even more important than that, he has identified that trust – so essential for everything we talk about in this book – isn't what happens in meetings. It's what happens between them. The corridor conversations checking in on family life, a significant event being looked forward to or having recently taken place, the sharing of confidences, hopes and fears.

It is in these moments that we make those connections and create trust. Not through the structured start and end of a virtual meeting. As diaries become full of back-to-back meetings, there is no time for the casual conversation or the pastoral care check in. You know what that looks like: those few moments at the end of a meeting where you've spotted someone isn't at their best and you take time to check in. When you've got to dial out of one piece of software and into another, and you haven't had a comfort break or eaten anything since you first logged on a few hours ago, you don't do this.

But you must. We all should. If our role as leaders and managers is to create an environment where people can be the best version of themselves, then we must find ways to encourage people to spend time with one another informally, as well as through formal meetings. If you can't get a mix of in-person and online time with your team, then create the space for one-to-one conversations which aren't about work per se, but are just about checking in. A safe space to say how people are feeling – what they are worried about, need and want. Feel confident as their leader to say that you don't have the answer, but help them find a solution by working with others.

We know that it can be soul destroying sitting on video calls and meetings all day. Mentally exhausting because you're not picking up on non-verbal cues. For some it creates a sense of insecurity from having their face on screen all the time. For others it could be feeling uncomfortable about an embarrassing interruption while working at home.[3] One study has shown that some people can feel intimidated if eye contact is held for too long and that meeting often online can lead to what psychologists call continuous partial attention.[4] How are you supporting your people with how they're feeling about this new world of work? How are you creating a safe space to talk about it on a one to one basis and as a team?

While there is no doubt about the potential for increased flexibility and quality of life from working at home, the boundaries between work and home have become inevitably blurred. The always-on working culture that was created with the recent advances in technology has been accelerated with an expectation that people are now available all of the time. Guard against expecting this of your team and others expecting it of you too. This will help you maintain your own wellbeing and that of your team, which we know is a key driver of productivity and high performance.

Flick back through this book and you'll find the tools you need. Generating commitment around team culture. Using feedback frequently and often. Running meetings in a way that is efficient and focused – creating a distinction between the purpose of a meeting and the small talk, rapport building, social capital creating activities that need to take place elsewhere.

Carving out thinking time to help you be better prepared. Making time to create purposeful interactions with stakeholders you need to influence. Being open to ambiguity and understanding the best way to navigate change – for yourself and others. These are as vital as ever, it's simply that we have different channels to use to now. Consider them new additions to your armoury, but the principles remain the same.

So go out there, and own your day.

Notes

[1] *The future of real estate*, Barclays special report, 22 September 2020.

[2] Simon Sinek speaking on trust when working virtually, www.youtube.com/watch?v=jVSYsINdMSo [accessed 15 December 2020].

[3] '5 reasons why Zoom meetings are exhausting', *The Conversation*, https://theconversation.com/5-reasons-why-zoom-meetings-are-so-exhausting-137404 [accessed 15 December 2020].

[4] Julia Sklar, '"Zoom fatigue" is taxing the brain. Here's why that happens', *National Geographic* (2020), www.nationalgeographic.co.uk/science-and-technology/2020/04/zoom-fatigue-is-taxing-the-brain-heres-why-that-happens [accessed 15 December 2020].

About the authors

Diana Marsland MA, BA (Hons), Fellow Higher Education Academy (FHEA)

Having gained a degree in Town Planning, Diana's first job was a media buyer in an advertising agency. Since that time, her varied career has taken her through marketing and project management in organizations as diverse as Halifax plc, the Foreign & Commonwealth Office, Fidelity Investments, Roffey Park Institute and the NHS. Working across all sectors, she has had line-management, executive and non-executive director roles and been trustee of a children's medical research charity. She lectures in Organizational Behaviour, delivers executive education, coaches and mentors.

While managing a project to merge two banks, observing people's reactions to the changes sparked an interest in organizational culture which was heightened when witnessing the effect of internet services in the 1990s. Since that time, she has had a particular interest in the impact of digital technology on work. She has undertaken research on the take-up of social networking in the workplace and spoken at conferences on social media and internal communication. She believes that managers' abilities are vastly underrated and that they will flourish with encouragement and support.

Julie Nerney MBA, Chartered Director (CDir), Fellow of the Institute of Directors (FIoD)

Julie was an accidental serial entrepreneur, starting 14 businesses in the UK and overseas, spanning sectors as diverse as a record label, health and fitness operations and a Polish speciality coffee company. Next came an interim career in business transformation. Assignments span complex change programmes, whole organizational turnarounds and high-profile projects, including a leadership role in the transport operation for the London 2012 Olympic and Paralympic Games. She has experience of every stage of organizational life, from start-up through to disposals and acquisitions, through dozens of Executive and CEO roles. She has a portfolio of Chair and NED roles for organizations with a social purpose, is a coach, mentor and guest lecturer, including providing insights for Oxford Saïd Business School's online leadership development programme.

Julie is struck by the commonality across the hundreds of organizations she has worked with. Regardless of why they exist, *how* teams approach their work is a far bigger driver of success than what they do. The what is important, but the *how* is the game changer. A passionate advocate for authentic, purposeful leadership, she loves to create cultures that allow individuals to be the best version of themselves.

Our grateful thanks to...

Alison Jones for inspiring us through her book and podcasts to believe this was possible, and then completing the journey with us by publishing the book.

Everyone at Practical Inspiration who helped us on the journey from beta draft to having this book in our hands.

Our beta readers Paul Taylor, Rob Calvert and James Hann for taking the time to read the draft and provide such wise and insightful feedback.

Natalie Adams for reading the draft and also for her wise insights and encouragement.

Chris Jones for his wisdom and the generous foreword.

Fiona Hiscocks Incledon of Thrive Change for facilitating one of our focus groups.

Every manager who gave so generously of their time in research interviews and responding to surveys.

To Collette Davis for the inspiration for the title of the book.

Our other halves, for their support and encouragement along the way.

Each other – we literally couldn't have done it alone!

Index

www.ingramcontent.com/pod-product-compliance
Lightning Source LLC
Jackson TN
JSHW011949131224
75386JS00042B/1642